Dr. Laura~

Wishing you fair winds
and happy adventures!

Carrie Bershee

Trading Ordinary...

For Extraordinary

Cruising Stories and Advice From A Mexico Sailing Adventure

by

CARRIE CALDWELL BERSHEE

Photos and Illustration by Bryan Bershee

authorHOUSE®

AuthorHouse™
1663 Liberty Drive, Suite 200
Bloomington, IN 47403
www.authorhouse.com
Phone: 1-800-839-8640

First published by AuthorHouse 6/24/2008

ISBN: 978-1-4343-8677-9 (sc)
ISBN: 978-1-4343-8678-6 (hc)

Library of Congress Control Number: 2008905436

Printed in the United States of America
Bloomington, Indiana

This book is printed on acid-free paper.

Permanently Temporary, just here for a little while
Definitely extraordinary, lovin' every new mile
Always underway, till the very last day
Never stationary
Enjoy life before it passes you by,
Because it's permanently temporary

Lyrics from "Permanently Temporary"
by Eric Stone

This book is dedicated to some very special people... To Bryan, for without your talents as a mariner and your willingness to indulge my wanderlust, this dream may never have been realized. And to our parents... it is because of your blessing and encouragement that we had the nerve to set sail. My heart overflows with love for you all.

Contents

Dream A Little Dream...

Stop and think for a minute.

What would you want to be doing right now – *this very instant* – if you could be doing anything you wanted?

Would you be sailing the tropical islands of the South Pacific? Would you be exploring the endless coves and beaches of the Pacific Northwest? Would you be preparing your boat for a circumnavigation?

Would you be doing something other than what you're doing right now?

Let me paint a picture for you. Imagine you are sailing your boat into a port you've been dreaming about for a long time. In all your planning, you have anticipated and envisioned your arrival in *this* port of call over and over again. The sky is bright blue and clear, the air is warm, the landscape is stunning. You and your crew feel a rush of pride, consumed for the moment by a sense of accomplishment for what you've managed to achieve. You're here! You did it! All the planning, hard work, and sacrifice have paid off. You feel like you're right where you're meant to be... the feeling is amazing.

Now let me paint that same picture for you in more vivid detail. Imagine you're sailing down the coast of Baja California, on a downhill run from Mag Bay to Cabo San Lucas. The overnight leg of your trip is heavenly, so flat and calm that you set up your laptop computer in the cockpit to watch movies. There seem to be millions and millions of stars in the midnight sky above you - so many, in fact, that looking at them for too long tends to make your eyes blur. The next day dawns bright and warm, and by mid-day you're so hot that you douse yourself with buckets of saltwater to cool off. You're thinking, "So this is winter in Mexico?"

By the time you arrive in Cabo San Lucas, you have to pinch yourself to make sure what you're experiencing isn't a dream. You're just off Lover's Beach, and to your surprise, you've been greeted by a gray whale. He's blowing and surfacing over and over, as if to welcome you, and it seems he has decided to escort you into the bay. Once you round Cabo's famous arches, gray and rugged, your senses are instantly overloaded by the sights in front of you: exquisite beachfront hotels, gigantic cruise ships, parasailors, sport fishing boats and sailboats as far as the eye can see. After three weeks of the barren and sparsely populated Baja coastline, this is a lot of stimulation for your brain to process. Admittedly, it may be even a bit more "civilization" than you generally prefer, but hey, *you could be at work right now.*

MAKING THE DREAM A REALITY

What has just been described here were actually the circumstances surrounding our arrival in Cabo San Lucas in December of 2005 on our 36' ketch, "Salty Dog." After taking three and a half weeks to meander down the Baja coast, with weather cooler than we would have liked and mechanical problems to boot, arriving in Cabo was hugely gratifying for my husband Bryan and me. Upon reaching the tip of the Baja peninsula, we were overcome by a huge sense of pride and accomplishment. We had come so far, and we were elated.

Many people we have met have been intrigued by the fact that we decided to go cruising now, in our 30's, in the midst of our careers and when most of our friends are having children. I suppose I could go on and on about why we did it, but the bottom line is that we decided to stop daydreaming and actually make our cruising dreams a reality. We had begun to feel stifled in our day-to-day lives, and we had arrived at a place mentally where we believed that the cruising lifestyle better fit our personalities and our belief systems than what we were living on a daily basis. We wanted to be self-reliant. We wanted to grow as individuals and as sailors, and we believed cruising would put us in an environment where we would be forced to do both. The events of our arrival in Cabo, as surreal as they may seem, reinforced for us that we had made the right decision.

You may be wondering if we just woke up one day and decided to sail away. As romantic as it would sound to say it was that easy, that isn't really the way it happened. We're human, and like most people, we were actually fairly embedded in our comfort zone of steady paychecks, proximity to family and friends, and the predictability of our daily routine. In all honesty, we worried if it was irresponsible to sell our home and our cars, and to give up our health insurance and monthly retirement contributions. Not having many assets, we knew if we decided to return home to California, it would be near impossible to get back into the overpriced housing market. We stressed about all the upgrades we would need to do to the boat to prep it for long-term cruising and all the money we would need to invest to do so. We both have many years of sailing experience, but naturally, we had doubts about our own skills and whether or not we were competent enough for this adventure.

So what finally convinced us that now was the time? What is it about Bryan and I that convinced us to untie the dock lines? Probably the single biggest motivating factor is that, as husband and wife, we shared a common dream. We were equally excited about what we wanted to do and we have tremendous faith in each other. Circumstances in our lives seemed to be handing us an opportunity to live out our dream *now*, and we were more fearful of missing out on our chance than of what it meant we would have to put on hold. We acknowledged that we didn't know everything there was to know, but we were okay with that. We were confident that we would learn along the way and grow from the mistakes we would surely make. We had already spent many weeks at a time together on our boat, and knew that we could live happily in a confined space and without the amenities of a land-based life. Our compatibility had already been proven.

The second biggest motivator for us was the support and encouragement (and sometimes envy) that we received from our friends and family. We were very fortunate in that regard. Our parents, our siblings, and our close friends urged us to fulfill our dream. They talked with us about our plans and showed interest in them, and they respected our decision to set sail. They all anxiously talked of visiting us in Mexico's beautiful ports and anchorages. Those of you who have considered cruising know that the support of your loved ones is hugely empowering.

Another motivator for Bryan and I was that we decided we wanted a more spontaneous lifestyle. As ironic as it sounds, we are both control freaks by nature. In our previous lives, we had a tendency to try to control our environment and most things in it. We craved predictability and orderliness. We liked to be guaranteed that our actions would have a positive outcome. I was neurotic about a clean house and keeping a daily to-do list, and Bryan obsessed about organizing his shed and the dock box! But for some reason, when it came to going cruising, we were ready to cast our compulsions aside and tackle all the unpredictability Mother Nature and King Neptune could throw at us. We were actually excited about testing our abilities and we looked forward to overcoming challenges. We wanted to rely on ourselves and no one else. We joked about our future life of less structure and eagerly anticipated fewer self-imposed "obligations."

Lastly, but equally as important, we set a departure date. And we told EVERYONE what it was! After that there was no way to back out. Having that departure date forces you to get busy on all those boat projects and upgrades that need to be completed. Overwhelming as it can be, it really is half the fun. You get to know your boat inside and out, and she really begins to feel like part of the family. One thing is for sure though - once you set a date, you start to feel like it's coming around the corner way too fast, while at the same time feeling like it couldn't come soon enough. It's simultaneously exciting *and* scary.

Once we had been cruising for a few months, did we have any regrets? Sure. We regretted not having lived more frugally in the months prior to our departure so that we would have had more money in the cruising kitty. We regretted having not purchased a wind generator, which would have proven useful many times over. We regretted not heading south with more spares, because Murphy's Law says that if you'd had a spare, the part that broke probably wouldn't have.

Was every day and every experience as wonderful as our landfall in Cabo San Lucas? No. Many days were fairly ordinary. Did we have issues to deal with, like bad weather and rough passages? Of course. Did we ever feel like going home? Maybe once or twice, but the feeling didn't last long. Has cruising changed us? We think it has changed us for the better. We're much better sailors than we were before. We're more patient. We're much more relaxed. And we feel so much healthier than we did before we left. Would we encourage others to do what we've done? Absolutely. If cruising is your dream and the opportunity presents itself, take it. You might not get another one. Whether you go for six months or six years, chances are you won't regret it.

CREW INFO:

Captain:	Bryan Bershee, age 34	Occupation: Middle school PE teacher
First Mate:	Carrie Bershee, age 32	Occupation: School counselor

CREW BIO:

Bryan and I both grew up sailing the waters off Southern California with our respective families. When we met in 1998 while working at the same middle school, we quickly realized that we shared a passion for the ocean and for sailing, and the rest, as they say, is history.

We were married in July 2000. Less than two years later we had purchased our own sailboat, an Ericson 27. Having a 6'3" husband and two active dogs, however, meant we quickly outgrew the 27-

footer. Convinced of our need for more space, Bryan and I began shopping for a bigger boat. The day the Pearson was hauled out for survey, the surveyor commented to us that the boat was sound enough to take us all the way to the South Pacific if we wanted. That was all we needed to hear to seal the deal on the Pearson and plant the seed for our future plans.

Bryan and I began to seriously talk about our desire to go cruising in January of 2004. At the time, we thought we could make it happen in six or seven years, after we had children and saved up a sufficient amount of money in the cruising fund. However, things don't always turn out the way you plan, and by late summer of 2004, we knew that an opportunity to set sail was staring us in the face, and we decided to go for it. As luck would have it, that June Bryan had been offered an opportunity to crew for a friend of ours on the schooner "Lifee P. Baker" on a voyage from Puerto Vallarta to Cabo San Lucas, and up the Sea of Cortez to La Paz. On the trip he gained a tremendous amount of experience and confidence, and came home more convinced than ever that now was the time for us to set sail. In August we attended a cruising seminar sponsored by Latitudes & Attitudes magazine, which sparked our confidence and excitement a little more. (And as if a sign from above that we were on the right track, we even won the grand prize in the raffle drawing – a week long bareboat charter in the British Virgin Islands!)

From the very first mention of our cruising plans, Bryan and I had nothing but support and encouragement from our families. We know what a rare thing this is, and we know we were truly blessed. We were also fortunate to have had a great deal of guidance and assistance from Bryan's dad, Dave. Dave spent many, many hours helping with mechanical fixes, installation of new equipment, and the unfortunate task of squeezing into tiny, cramped little spaces better accessed by someone less than 5 feet tall. To him, we are eternally grateful. While there was no doubt that we all would miss each other while Bryan and I are away, we knew that both sets of parents, as well as Bryan's brother and my sister, would come to visit us along the way. The fact that our loved ones encouraged us to fulfill our dream means more to us than they know.

Bryan and I were not alone on our trip, however. We were accompanied on this amazing adventure by our two dogs, Fletcher and Sadie. Fletcher, for whom the boat is named, is an adorably goofy middle-aged Weimaraner. Sadie is a protective and adventurous spaniel mix who gives a whole new level of meaning to the term "Mama's girl". Fletcher and Sadie keep us laughing and keep us sane, and we were so glad to have them along. They both love the ocean and love sailing. If they could talk, Bryan and I are convinced that the dogs would tell us they are happiest living on the boat and being with their owners 24/7. They get to swim, hike, lay around in the sun or on the deck under the sun awning, and play with other dogs on the beach. Life is good for these two mutts! We know our trip would not have been nearly as fun or memorable without them.

Welcome Aboard!

ABOUT SALTY DOG...

Salty Dog is a Pearson 365 ketch-rigged sailboat, built and launched in Rhode Island in 1979 by Pearson Yachts. Purchased by The Bershee's in 2003, her home port is now Los Angeles, California.

ABOUT THE NAME...

We chose the vessel name Salty Dog in "honor" of our oldest dog, Fletcher. When he was younger, Fletcher, the cross-eyed Weimaraner, had a habit of falling off the dock, the boat, and the dinghy, and into the water. Because we always seemed to have a wet and salty dog aboard the boat, the name was an easy choice.

ABOUT LIFE ABOARD SALTY DOG...

Accommodations: The main sleeping accommodations aboard Salty Dog are in the v-berth. Additionally, there is a pilot berth in the main salon and two settees that can be used in a pinch as single berths. The cockpit is extremely large for a boat this size, and can easily sleep two people outside under the stars in nice weather. The head has a manual-flush toilet, sink, medicine cabinet, lots of storage, and a large stall shower.

Galley: Salty Dog's galley boasts a propane two-burner stove/oven, a deep sink, a large deep locker for dry goods storage, a fairly large freezer, and a large top-loading refrigerator. We carry two propane tanks, mounted in a rear lazaret, to avoid ever running out of propane in a remote location where we can't easily get more. While the rail-mount propane BBQ isn't actually *in* the galley, it is nonetheless a very important piece of galley equipment and gets used regularly. Bryan has done a significant amount of customization to the galley to make it more user-friendly... a new Technautics cold-plate refrigeration system replaced the old AdlerBarbour unit, and at the same time he modified the existing icebox design so that we could have a dedicated freezer. A spice rack has been added to the countertop behind the stove to free up space in the cupboard. Extra shelving has been added under the sink, as well as a custom-designed knife rack mounted on the inside of one of the cabinet doors.

Engine: The engine is a Westerbeke 40 hp and is original to the boat. Not very fast, but very reliable! The heat exchanger was rebuilt in 2004 when it became clogged, and the alternator was replaced in August 2005.

Sails: Salty Dog is a ketch and therefore has more sail area than a traditional sloop rigged sailboat. We purchased a new main sail, mizzen sail, and slide track system in 2004 from Quantam sails and are very happy with them. They are made of heavy sail cloth for heavy weather, and the main boasts three reef points while the mizzen boasts one. Additionally, we have a roller-furling jib and a beautiful hand-me-down spinnaker (from Carrie's parents) in a pattern reminiscent of the American flag.

Power/electricity: The old set of two house batteries were removed the summer before we departed, and a new set of four golf cart house batteries and one dedicated starter battery were installed. A Xantrex 1800 inverter/charger was also installed, and allows us to operate small appliances like a coffee pot and a toaster. A Xantrex Link 1000 monitoring system now tells us how many amp hours we have used as well as how many we have in reserve, and lets us monitor how well the batteries are charging. While most everything except the hot water heater can be run off of 12-volt, Salty Dog also has 110 volt capabilities when plugged in to shore power at a marina or to our Honda 2000 generator.

<u>Tankage</u>: We hold 50 gallons of diesel fuel and 100 gallons of water. Additionally, we ripped out our old 15 gallon holding tank and converted a larger, unused water tank in the bow to our current holding tank.

<u>Communications</u>: Salty Dog has a newly installed ICOM M422 VHF radio with remote mike at the helm, an ICOM M32 handheld, waterproof VHF radio, and a Single Side Band radio.

<u>Electronics</u>: All electronics aboard Salty Dog were new for this trip. Furuno 1623 Radar. Garmin 192C Chart plotter. Raymarine depth sounder and knot meter. Raymarine ST6001 linear drive autopilot. Electronics aboard which are not new but still come in handy are a Garmin handheld GPSMap 76 and a Garmin stationary-mount GPS 75 at the chart table. For entertainment, we have an AM/FM stereo with CD player and indoor/outdoor speakers, an IPOD with all of our favorite music, and an IBM T42 laptop computer for watching our collection of DVDs and keeping our website current, as well as communicating with friends and loved ones via email.

<u>Watermaker</u>: A "Little Wonder" watermaker was installed by Village Marine. Totally modular, it fits in the bilge and takes up hardly any room. One of our biggest purchases, this amazing piece of equipment converts salt water into drinking water more pure than the bottled water we buy at the grocery store. Producing 6 gallons an hour, our watermaker guarantees that we will always have safe water for drinking, cooking, and showering.

<u>Ground Tackle</u>: Salty Dog carries a 45 pound CQR and a 22 pound Danforth, as well as 100 feet of chain and 150 feet of rode. On our trip we never once used the Danforth, relying solely on the CQR and it never let us down. Often times in the same conditions in which other boats would drag anchor, we tended to stay put. We also carry 30 feet of chain and 140 feet of rode for the rare occasion in which we set a stern anchor.

Safety: Salty Dog is equipped with an EPIRB, flares, harnesses, life jackets, a life ring, Zodiac 6-person life raft, and a MOB (man overboard pole).

Dinghy/Outboard: Another big but very important purchase was a new Caribe 9-foot RIB dinghy and a Tohatsu 6hp outboard engine. While cruising and living aboard, a dinghy is like your SUV, and you need one that is reliable. Ours is affectionately nicknamed the "SUD" (Sport Utility Dinghy).

Miscellaneous: Some of the equipment that is hard to categorize but that has nonetheless made our lives more comfortable are 12-volt fans in the v-berth, head, and galley; custom cockpit cushions from C-Cushions that are tough enough to withstand the dogs nails; stainless steel MarTek dinghy davits; custom stainless steel cockpit railings (which replaced the original life lines).

Many, many people helped us equip and customize our boat for this adventure and we will forever be grateful. We are especially indebted to Anthony Mattera, formerly of ICON Industries in San Pedro and currently the owner of South Bay Marine, for his guidance and friendship; Shawn of Muller Marine in San Pedro for his help with the propane conversion and lots of other helpful tips along the way; and John Rice of Wilmington for his assistance with customizing the installation of the linear drive autopilot. Thank you also to all of our A Dock extended family for their tireless dockside supervision, wisdom, and encouragement.

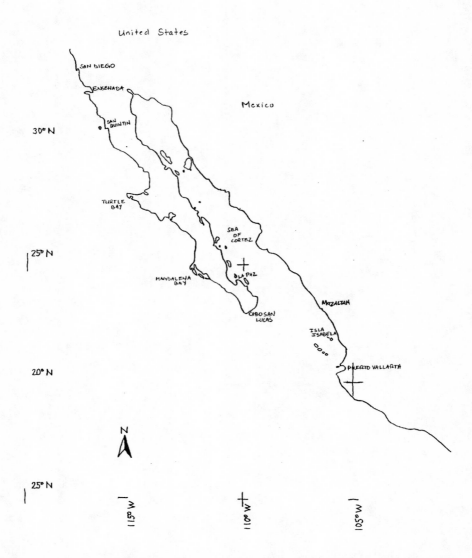

United States

SAN DIEGO

ENSENADA

Mexico

30° N

SAN
QUINTIN

TURTLE
BAY

SEA
OF
CORTEZ

25° N

MAGDALENA
BAY

LA PAZ

CABO SAN
LUCAS

MAZATLAN

ISLA
ISABELA

20° N

PUERTO VALLARTA

N

25° N

115° W

110° W

105° W

Disclaimer: All coordinates cited in this publication are approximate and should not be used for navigational purposes.

Chapter 1

Are we ready for this?!?!

B RYAN AND I HAD BEEN scheming and planning for quite a while for a way to be able to take some time off and go cruising on our sailboat. We always figured our "dream" would have to wait until we had accomplished more and were more financially "set". But then things started happening, both personal and professional, causing us to question the logic of waiting so long.

After a year of rapidly worsening health, my dear grandmother, "Grandma Grump," had passed away. She and I had always been close, but since her move back to my hometown after the death of my grandfather a couple of years earlier, we had been able to spend a lot more time together and had grown even closer. Bryan and I had hesitation about going cruising when she was in such poor health. Then, in the last few months of my grandmother's life, I too was diagnosed with some health problems that ultimately required major surgery and a six week recovery. Those two events reinforced for Bryan and me that life is precious and is often too short. The California real estate market was on fire, and if we sold our house, we could have enough money to fulfill our dream now instead of ten or twenty years from now.

So, in the spring of 2005, our house in the mountains of Southern California was put up for sale and sold after only 24 hours on the market. Two days later we resigned from our jobs as junior high school educators. We had a 30 day escrow and had to be out of the house by June 15th, which turned out to be a bigger undertaking than we had planned on. With me still recovering from surgery, I was no help when it came to all the heavy lifting, so thank goodness for Bryan's dad, Dave, who came to our rescue. Let me tell you, moving out of a 1500 square foot house and on to a 36' sailboat is no easy task. You have no idea how hard it is to pack up a whole house full of stuff when you aren't just putting it in a Uhaul and moving it to another house, but instead are downsizing and liquidating. It literally took us 10 days to do it all, as well as 5 trips to the dump, 3 trips to local thrift stores, and more trips than I can count to our new makeshift storage unit in Dave and Barb's basement at their house in Lake Arrowhead.

In the weeks after quitting our jobs and selling our home, we spent a good deal of time and energy enjoying our new status as "retirees." We boasted of our new freedom to anyone who would listen, and found great satisfaction in their envy, even though deep down we knew we were only *temporarily* retired.

As soon as we were out of our house, we headed to our boat, which was docked in Cabrillo Marina in San Pedro, in the port of Los Angeles. We needed to move it to Newport the very next day in anticipation of a captain's licensing course Bryan was to start that following week and we would be staying in a guest slip there while he attended his classes. We knew having the license would decrease the cost of our insurance, and hoped it might look good on a resume should we try to get work along the way. We stayed on the boat in Newport for a total of twelve days. Bryan passed his licensing course with flying colors. His score of 97% was much deserved, as he studied relentlessly for 12 straight days.

Our hope was to then return to San Pedro for the final 4-6 weeks of boat projects. If everything had gone as planned, we would have spent August and September at Catalina Island, twenty miles west of Los Angeles, and then we would head south to San Diego in early October. But that was *if* everything had gone as planned.

By August 1st our boat upgrades were nowhere close to being completed. We were SO naïve to think that we could get everything done in one month. Looking at it now, it seems so obvious, which leaves us to wonder why no one brought it to our attention earlier! Surely the saltier boaters and more seasoned among us recognized that with our incredibly long "to do" list, we would need much longer than one month.

Anyhow, there we were in San Pedro, still tackling boat projects through the month of August. We really enjoyed our time there despite how impatient we felt to get everything done and get the heck out of dodge. Our dock was so friendly and there was always something going on or someone with whom we could visit. Dennis, one of our favorite "stink pot" power boat-owner friends, said to us one afternoon while watching us work, "It would be okay with me if you guys were stuck here a little longer. We all like having you around." It had really begun to feel a lot like family there, and we were sure it would be fairly difficult to say goodbye when the time came.

Thankfully, we did manage to get two of the big projects done, namely the new battery bank and monitoring system, and the watermaker. These two additions really made *me* happy, as now I would be able to take showers without feeling guilty about water consumption, and because the inverter that was installed along with the new batteries allowed me to use my coffeepot and a toaster. Small conveniences when living on land, HUGE conveniences on a boat!

In late August, Bryan and I finally gave ourselves permission to take a few days off from boat projects and get out of the marina. "Break the concrete away from the hull," as my husband likes to say. Catalina Island, conveniently located off the coast of Southern California, is a mecca for SoCal boaters. With the little city of Avalon and its tourist amenities on the east end, and numerous anchorages, and popular diving and fishing spots sprinkled up and down the coast, the island draws mariners and outdoor enthusiasts all year long. This particular weekend was my mom's birthday, and the family tradition is to gather in Two Harbors, at the west end of the island, and make a weekend event out of our celebration. This year's group consisted of my parents, me and Bryan, my sister Christie and her boyfriend Casey, and family friends Nicole and Andre.

The good times started off with a bang on Friday morning when we got a call from my Uncle Dennis, my dad's brother, that he and his entire family were on a dive boat anchored at Ship Rock, just outside the harbor. What fortunate coincidence! We decided to take Salty Dog off the mooring and motor out to their location. When we concluded that we couldn't get too close to the dive boat because they had divers in the water, their captain was nice enough to deliver them all out to our boat in his skiff. Mom and Dad, Bryan and I, Dennis and Vicki, Matt, Zack, and Tara sat in the cockpit visiting for a little over an hour before they had to leave us. While we all would have liked to have visited longer, it was still a nice surprise and a great start to the weekend.

After lunch aboard with Mom and Dad, there was a little boat washing to be done before the dinner hour, when Christie, Casey and Nicole were expected to arrive on the ferry. Fortunately, we also were able to squeeze a leisurely dinghy ride into the afternoon's activities. (What's that old saying about "all work and no play...") When the rest of the gang arrived later that day, Mom prepared dinner for all of us aboard Andre's boat. In keeping with a somewhat informal tradition in Two Harbors, the evening concluded with many cocktails and much dancing at the patio bar.

Saturday was pretty mellow, with breakfast served aboard Salty Dog for everyone, then some swimming and naps before we had to catch the shuttle to the "Airport In The Sky," the island's small private airport located high up in the interior, for the Catalina-style BBQ and music they put on a few times each summer. The extremely clear skies and extraordinary visibility made for an especially nice evening – especially for Nicole, who had never been to the interior of the island before. The visibility was so good that we could see the skyscrapers of Los Angeles almost 30 miles away.

The whole gang was able to share lunch together on the patio of the Harbor Reef Restaurant Sunday morning before Christie, Casey, Nicole, and Andre had to go home on the ferry. Once we said our goodbyes, we did little else for the rest of the day other than read, take a dinghy ride, and go out to dinner, again at the Harbor Reef restaurant, the only restaurant at that end of the island.

Monday morning was difficult for Bryan and me because we really didn't want to go home. While the events of the last few days hadn't been all that out of the ordinary for a family trip to the island, we were again reminded of how much we love Two Harbors and the pace of life there. Bryan said to me, "I really don't want to leave today."

"I know. Technically, we are retired, so we don't have to leave if we don't want to," I replied with a grin.

We schemed about how we could justify staying just one more day, but ultimately gave in to the pull of the "to-do" list. So with our heavy hearts we headed back to San Pedro and left a place that feels so much like home to us.

The heaviness in my heart left me questioning what is it about a place that makes it so hard to leave? I always get this feeling, this emotional tug-of-war, when it's time to leave the island. Even though I have had to do it hundreds of time since my childhood, it seems to be a lot more complicated than just the "end of vacation blues" that a lot of people get at the end of their holiday. I think it's not so much about the time off from work and life as we would otherwise know it, and more about the place - *this place*. For me, maybe it's because I've been coming here all of my life and so many happy memories were made here, that it has a feeling of "home" for me. Maybe, too, it's the simplicity of life on the island...freedom from complications and obligations associated with life in the rest of Southern California.

On that particular day, I found myself trying to find a justification for the sentimentality I was feeling as Bryan and I headed back to San Pedro. We knew we had to get back. There were still many projects to be done before our November departure. And while the truth of this was very real to us both, I suppose it was nice to have the burden of those chores lifted from us for awhile, even knowing that their completion would put us that much closer to our goal.

Maybe this all sounds a bit overly sentimental. But have you ever experienced a place that just feels so right and comfortable to you that you know it is somewhere you are supposed to be? More and more that is how Bryan and I feel about Catalina. The place just seems to compliment our personalities and the laid back way we want to live our lives. Bryan and I, and the rest of you who have had the chance to spend quality time at Catalina Island, are very fortunate, as it is one of California's last unspoiled places.

Chapter 2

King Neptune's First Test

$\mathcal{F}$ROM AN EMAIL TO FAMILY and friends dated October 17th, 2005:

Well, it's official. We've done it. We've said good-bye to all our friends on the dock, turned in our gate keys and parking passes, and vacated our slip. Without a slip to go home to, I guess we're really cruising now!

After a few errands in the morning and a couple of last minute tasks, we were ready to cast off the docklines around noon. However, the gang from the dock came by to say farewell, and because we all became a bit emotional, the process took a little while. We were given a send off by Bryan's parents Dave and Barb, Leon and Leticia, Rick and Jeanelle, Mike, Jonathon, Anthony, Dennis, John, Mike and Sue, and Little Tony.

We had a warm and fairly uneventful crossing to Avalon, where we had decided to spend the night because my parents were there for the annual jazz festival. We were not able to get a mooring inside as the harbor was full, and ended up on a can in Descanso next to the Casino seawall. That night we celebrated our upcoming adventure and retiree status with cocktails and appetizers at the Portofino. Our intention was to rendezvous with Mom and Dad after their concert let out, but it got to be pretty late and we were tired, so we went back to the boat to turn in, agreeing that we would meet them the next morning for breakfast instead.

We woke Sunday morning around 5 AM to strong, howling winds and big, rolling swells. The unexpected storm was pretty uncomfortable, and the dogs, especially little Sadie, were really nervous. After getting up long enough to peer out the hatches and see how ugly it was outside, we crawled back in our bunk and tried to go back to sleep. No such luck. By 5:45 AM we were up for good. I was having flashbacks to a time when I was about ten years old, and my family was on our sailboat "Charley Girl" on a mooring inside Avalon when similar conditions arose. While my parent's boat rode it out okay, a few other boats closer to the beach ended up on the rocks that day. I remember Harbor Patrol pounding on the side of the boat around 6:00 AM, telling us to get dressed, get off the boat, and get to shore. Pretty scary for a little kid.

I was really nervous now because we were so close to the seawall. We decided to get dressed and turn on the VHF radio. It was then that we heard a report of a 50' ketch near us who had broken its mooring line. Calls for help to Harbor Patrol were being met with a response that they already had so many distress calls that boaters were pretty much on their own. "Put out some extra fenders," was all they were able to suggest. Then the swells started breaking under us. It felt like we were inside the barrel of a washing machine. Because we were so close to the seawall, Bryan and I decided that the smartest thing to do at that moment would be to vacate our mooring and get a little more room between us and the rocks. This was no easy task when the boat was bucking back in forth in the swells like a bull in a rodeo. But, by 6:30 AM we dropped the mooring and were headed out of Descanso.

As luck would have it, as soon as we cleared that last row of moorings, the engine died. Despite a couple of desperate attempts, Bryan couldn't get it started again. Then it started to rain. The wind was howling, probably up to about 25 knots. We stared drifting back towards the moorings and the other boats. Bryan rushed up on deck to raise some sails, but there was way too much wind to get the main up, so we went with jib – anything to get us moving away from the other boats!

Because of the direction of the wind, we couldn't go around the east end of the island like we wanted, to the backside of the island where it would be more protected from the wind. So we sailed west, past Long Point, towards Two Harbors. Although we were both feeling nauseous from the seas, a few too many cocktails the night before, and no breakfast, I somehow managed to go down below and retrieve our foul weather gear. The boat was a disaster. We left the mooring so quickly that we didn't have time to adequately stow everything. Magazines and books were on the floor. Clothes were everywhere. Thank God the laptop computer was still where it was supposed to be, but I moved it to the protection of the v-berth anyway. The dogs, although probably a little freaked out and definitely needing to go to the bathroom, seemed to be doing surprisingly well. Unlike us, at least they were dry!

So on we sailed, in the rain, with huge following seas and about 30 knots of wind. The boat, thankfully, handled like a dream. As we neared Two Harbors, we toyed with the idea of pulling in, but then began to hear on the VHF all the problems they too were having because of the weather - boats dragging on their moorings, dingies capsizing, the works. Not knowing what was wrong with the engine, how long it would take to fix, or how long the crazy weather would stick around, we concurred that Cat Harbor was the safest place to be. Cat Harbor, on the backside of the island, is considered one of the safest harbors on the entire West Coast, and would definitely be the most comfortable place to ride out bad weather.

By 10:00 AM, we were at the west end. The seas started to calm down. The sun came out. The wind let up a little. Good news, right? By 11:00 AM, we could see Cat Head, the entrance to Cat Harbor, about five miles ahead.

AND THEN THE WIND DIED.

We tacked and started heading away from the island to pick up any little puff of breeze, which worked for a bit, until that breeze became intermittent, and we decided to tack again. And there we sat. We could see where we wanted to be, but despite all our efforts, we couldn't get there. So frustrating!

At 2:30 PM, I was ready to call Vessel Assist and let them tow us the rest of the way. I don't know whether to blame it on stubborn pride or courteousness, but Bryan argued that we shouldn't make someone come all that way, when after all, we were so close. I countered with, "But that's their job, and that's what we pay our membership for!" But he's the captain, and in the end, he makes the decision. So instead, my ever-determined-not-to-be- beaten husband rigged a bridle to the bow of the boat, and towed us the rest of the way with the dinghy. Yes, you heard me right! He got in the dinghy, and towed our 36', 10 ton sailboat for almost two hours with a 6 horsepower outboard.

Once inside the harbor, Harbor Patrol came out to meet us and towed us to a mooring. That was around 4:30 PM. After we were secure on the mooring, the plan was to take the dogs ashore, bring them back to the boat, and then take ourselves to the restaurant for a warm, hearty meal. Like I said, that was the plan. However, on the way back to the boat after walking the dogs, the heavens opened up again and it began to POUR. Neither one of us really felt like spending more time in the cold rain than we had to, so instead we opted to cook aboard. Eggs, hash browns, toast — comfort food- and we hadn't had breakfast yet that day anyway. While we contemplated watching a movie, we knew we were too exhausted to stay awake through it, and instead crawled into bed at 7:30! After all, we hoped the next day would be busy with engine repairs, and we wanted to be well rested.

Wouldn't you know it? We woke Monday morning to more rain, and it continued raining most of the day, making engine repair a little difficult since our engine is partially accessed from the lazarettes in our cockpit. Our couple of trips to shore with the dogs left us soaking wet. It sure will be nice when the rain stops and we can dry out our boat and our soggy gear.

Having gotten some rest, and having had time to review the events of the past 24 hours, Bryan and I are actually kind of glad this happened to us. It was a test of our skills, our boat, and our resolve, and we feel pretty good about how we handled it. Whatever happened with the engine probably had a lot to do with how much we were getting tossed around and all the junk that then had the opportunity to clog the fuel filters. The boat, however, handled great, and our confidence in her continues to grow. Although we're sure we'll have to deal with more bad *weather and mechanical problems along the way, we're both satisfied that we've passed King Neptune's first test.*

Two Harbors, while a favorite place of many mariners, is not exactly a shoppers paradise. It offers very limited supplies and spare parts, especially the kind of spare parts boaters down on their luck (like us) might need in the event you have to actually repair something while you're there. So we were extremely relieved when we were joined on Friday afternoon by Bryan's parents, who had arrived from San Pedro aboard their sailboat, "Scooter." Dave and Barb, in addition to joining us for Two Harbors' annual "Cruiser's Weekend," delivered the engine parts Bryan had ordered from our friend Anthony back in San Pedro. We didn't attempt any boat repairs Friday evening, and instead went into "town" to hear Eric Stone playing on the patio of the Harbor Reef restaurant and hung out with the Bershee clan, which included Bryan's brother, Mike, and his girlfriend, Amy, who was visiting the island for the first time.

Saturday morning we woke to more cold and yucky weather, drizzly and gray. After breakfast on Dave and Barb's boat, Bryan began working on the engine. He had to send Mike on a parts run, to no avail – not much in the way of boat parts to be had in this tiny island town. Being the mechanical wizards that they are, and not ones to be easily defeated by challenges such as these, the Bershee men put their heads together to come up with a temporary fix, and then with a final suggestion from Dave, the engine fired right up! We were so relieved. Of course this called for celebratory cocktails, lovingly provided by Mike and Amy. They had come up with some crazy concoction of wine coolers and vodka, but after a day like the one we had just had, who could complain? It was the thought that counted!

Saturday night we went to the cruiser's party and BBQ on the beach, where Eric Stone was performing again. Bryan and I really enjoy his music, and made a point of telling him that his song "Permanently Temporary" is one of our favorites. Not surprisingly, by the end of the night Amy was smitten with the island, and we were pleased to be part of her inaugural Catalina experience.

15

After walking the dogs Sunday morning, we again had a nice breakfast aboard "Scooter." My mother-in-law is a great cook, and any time, under any conditions, can put out a spread of food that would put a lot of professional chefs to shame. After filling our bellies once again, the two boats then departed Cat Harbor together around 11:30 A.M. After we rounded the West End, Scooter turned toward San Pedro and we headed for Two Harbors for the night.

On Monday, Bryan and I woke early (for "retired" folks) – 6:45 A.M. – wanting to get an early start for our eight hour sail to Dana Point. However, after breakfast, walking the dogs, visiting with our friend Mike, and getting fuel, we didn't actually leave until 9:30. The crossing was a little cold and drizzly at first, but once we were about an hour past Long Point, the sun came out partially. It was a really quiet sail… I read, we listened to music, and trolled a fishing line. Other than about a 30 second tease from a thresher shark, we had no action on the line.

We got in to Dana Point around 6:00 P.M., and anchored in the West Basin under the tall bluffs that shelter the harbor, right near the Marine Institute and their two tall ships. There was only one other sailboat on anchor, a Beneteau First named Ohana, a boat we would later learn was headed to San Diego for the start of the Baja Ha Ha rally to Mexico. The harbor was flat and calm, and it quickly seemed as if it was at least ten degrees warmer than the island had been. We took the dogs to shore, had showers and a simple dinner aboard, and called it a night.

Bryan and I wanted to spend time in Dana Point prior to our departure for a few reasons. For one, at the time Bryan's brother was living only 20 minutes away, and we really wanted to see him a bit more before we set sail. Also, my parents kept their boat in Dana Point, and together with Bryan's parents, had planned a going away party for us on their dock. Together our families threw us an amazing bon voyage party, complete with live music by Don Ross, our wonderful boat broker, the guy who sold us Salty Dog. Don is a boat broker by day, one man rock-and-roll party by night. He set up his equipment on the bow of the Charley Girl, and entertained us with songs from Jimmy Buffet, Neil Diamond, and other of our favorite artists. So many of our good friends were there, even people we hadn't seen in ages and others who really surprised us by attending. We realized how blessed we truly are to have such great people to call friends.

Knowing that we were now really close to departing the country, we had gotten to feeling a bit sappy, wanting to be sure we found a way to tell our parents everything we were thinking and feeling before we said "adios." It wasn't like we weren't ever going to see them again, but still, what we were about to do was a big deal. So Bryan and I each decided to write our parents a letter that we gave to them after the party.

October 29, 2005

Mom & Dad:

I just wanted to take a make sure that I took the time to say thank you before this day ends. Without you two as my parents, there is no way I would be leaving in a few days for Mexico, about to live out what so many people only dream of. I truly believe that my life has been taking a course that has led me to this very moment, to this very opportunity. And while you may not take any of the credit for yourselves, it is important to me that you know that this journey has so much to do with you and your influence on my life.

In my childhood, you charted a course for adventure for me by exposing me to your love of the ocean and sailing, to traveling, and to experiencing other cultures and parts of the world. I overheard your conversations about exotic times while living in Jamaica, as well as your conversations about "cruising," a fantastical concept to a little girls imagination. You taught me songs about the ocean, allowed me to learn how to fish (even when I didn't like cleaning what I caught!), and didn't disown me when I accidentally committed the British Seagull to the depths of Newport Harbor. You showed me how to sleep in the cockpit under the stars, and how to enjoy a good barbeque on the beach. You let me bring my own friends to the marina and to the island, letting me experience the happiness that came from sharing my love of those places with them. You let Christie and I spend time around your "boat friends," and to this day I can say that they were and are some of the finest people I have ever known. Mostly though, you showed me by your example the importance of finding something you love to do as a family, and spending quality time together doing it.

Our family ventured to many exciting places: the Olympics in Canada and Los Angeles, to many beautiful and important spots all across the United States, and we even spent time watching the whales migrate through Mexico. As I got older, you began to step back a little, enabling me to chart my own course more and more. You allowed me to pursue my growing love of travel, and sent me to Mexico, England, Wales and all over Europe. You even allowed a college Spring Break trip to Baja (in a station wagon that belonged to a friend of yours, no less!) While so many people go through life feeling bitter about all they didn't get to do in their childhood, I have never been one of those people.

Tied only with having found my soul mate in Bryan, my greatest blessing in life was to have been born to such amazing parents. You have always shared your dreams and loves with me, and supported my own. Now, as Bryan and I chart our own course for this amazing adventure we are about to embark upon, here you are supporting, encouraging, and mentoring us. Thank you for all you have done in my life to help me get to this day, as well as for the celebration you are hosting for Bryan and me. It goes without saying that am going to miss you terribly, but I wouldn't have it any other way. It is only proof of the depth of my love for you both. (Your visit in December will help, but don't hesitate to plan another trip for the Spring!)

I have so much on my heart and I have no idea how to end this letter, so let me just say this: I am overwhelmingly proud to be your daughter, you will be in my thoughts and prayers each and every day, and I love you.

Carrie

୬

October 29, 2005

Dear Mom & Dad:

I cannot begin to express the thanks for all the many years of happiness, joy, and encouragement that you both have given me. Mom- from making the cheesecake squares for every football game, to sitting in the driveway talking to me for many hours, while I sat there and smoked my pipe. Dad- for all the encouragement at the games, telling me to go harder with the throw. Now with the adventure of a lifetime in front of Carrie and me, you guys have given so much to helping out with the fixing of the boat, advice on mounting locations of certain new electronics, to always being there when we needed help.

It was hard saying goodbye to all the extended family on A Dock, but saying goodbye to ones family is much more difficult. The one good thing is that you guys get to come down and visit us in locations we used to only read about in the magazines. Now we'll get to visit them first hand.

In finishing this letter I have no clue how it should end. So, I'm not going to end it, but open a whole new chapter in our lives with this wonderful adventure. I love you guys so much. See you soon in exotic places.

Love,
Your Son,
Bryan

After deciding to push back our departure by one day in order to accomplish a few more last minute projects, we left Dana Point on November 1st at 4:45 AM for Mission Bay, just north of San Diego harbor. Our trip was glorious. We left under a star-filled sky, which quickly turned into an amazing sunrise. We were anchored in Mariner's Cove in Mission Bay by 2:00 P.M. This gave us time to take the dogs for a romp on the beach and take a dinghy ride before barbequing cheeseburgers for dinner. After dinner we watched a movie in the cockpit under a starry sky. As the movie ended, I said to Bryan, "If we have too many more days like this, we may never go home!"

The next morning we weighed anchor at 9:45 AM, bound for Shelter Island in San Diego Bay. Three and a half hours later, we were tied up to the Customs dock to request a guest slip. There are only 30 guest slips and almost all of them were full. Because the guest docks don't allow for advance reservations, we felt fortunate to get the last assignment. And unbelievably, the cost was only $10.50 a night. We were assigned slip #26, right next to John and Donna on Kohilo, whom we had met in Cat Harbor a couple of weeks earlier. We immediately noticed that most of the boats were cruising sailboats. In fact, on our first day at the guest docks, we only spotted one power boat. In talking to the other boaters, we discovered that at least 75% of them were also headed to Mexico.

Every year in late summer and early fall, hundreds of private vessels from as far away as Alaska make their way down the Pacific Coast, ultimately bound for the warmer climates and inviting cruising grounds of Mexico and points farther south. These boats congregate in San Diego, a huge natural harbor with a great climate and a multitude of services for boaters. San Diego is also the starting point for the Baja Ha Ha cruisers rally that heads south each year at the end of October.

Shelter Island is consequently a haven for boaters, so being there was very convenient, although it was a bit of a walk from the guest docks to the business district. There are more marine stores and chandleries in this neighborhood than I can keep count of. We were able to get things we needed at Downwind Marine, Phantom Marine (Furuno dealer), Seabreeze (charts and nautical books), and West Marine. (It is interesting to note that the West Marine on Shelter Island is the biggest on the west coast and really caters to cruisers. For instance, they have computers with free internet usage so you can check the weather, your email, etc., as well as printers and copy machines that are also free to use). Additionally, we purchased our Mexican fishing licenses through Dona Jenkins Maritime Services on Shelter Island, which saved us from the hassle of having to take a taxi into downtown.

On Friday, our last night at the docks and also my birthday, some of the ladies on the dock had planned an impromptu dock party. Having found out it was my birthday, they surprised me with a cake, candles, and a hearty rendition of "Happy Birthday." It was all very fun, but we were off to bed early because 4:00 AM was quickly approaching and we had a border to cross.

Chapter 3

San Diego to Cabo San Lucas
No Turning Back Now!

Ensenada

WE LEFT THE SHELTER ISLAND guest docks at 4:15 AM- so early, but we didn't want to pull into Ensenada in the dark. We passed two large cruise ships on our way out of the harbor, and two smaller boats as well. Lots of activity for such an early hour! Again, we had an uneventful trip south, other than some large following seas that Sadie didn't seem to like too much. It was during this phase of the trip that we decided we loved our

ENSENADA

31° 50.5 N
116° 37.4 W

Population: 180,000

Highlight: *Ensenada is the first major port south of the U.S.-Mexico border, and is the most common place for cruisers heading south to officially enter into the country. Additionally, fuel and a multitude of services can be obtained here.*

new autopilot and the comfort it gave us underway. In fact, we gave some serious thought to naming it "amigo." Ultimately, we settled on the named "Dana," though, in honor of Dana Point, the place where Bryan finally got the autopilot to work correctly.

We crossed the international line at 9:45 AM and were officially in Mexico, although still many hours from Ensenada. Around 5:30 PM we arrived at Marina Coral, a nice marina and hotel complex almost three miles north of Ensenada's main harbor entrance. It was dusk so we could still make out the breakwater and marina entrance, but just barely. I certainly wouldn't want to enter this harbor in the dark. It is a very small, narrow passage. The marina, however, is wonderful. After showers and all the other post-passage rituals (like straightening up the boat and walking the dogs), we had a fabulous dinner in the restaurant to celebrate our arrival in foreign waters. We explored the grounds of Hotel Coral, and decided the pools and jacuzzi (both indoor and outdoor) would need to be visited in the next day or two.

On Sunday, we hung new life line netting that we purchased in San Diego. We hoped it would give the dogs a little more security on deck and give us greater peace of mind when they decide they need to stretch their legs under way. I have undertaken one doggy-overboard drill already in recent times, and I didn't want to do another one if I didn't have to! In the afternoon we had the jacuzzi all to ourselves, and indulged in a few adult beverages while relaxing. All in all, a pretty mellow day.

It had been arranged for a driver from the hotel to take us to Customs and Immigration the following day. We had been told to be ready at 9:00 AM, so of course we were. When we checked in at the marina office, however, we were told that the driver was running late and we wouldn't leave now until 10:00 AM. We killed time looking through the hotel store and had something to drink in the restaurant before checking back in. At 10:00 AM, we were informed that we would need to wait another 30 minutes, as the driver still had not arrived. Bryan and I chuckled to ourselves and decided this was our first lesson learned in "manana land"... it doesn't do any good to be in a hurry.

Customs was a breeze, and in total, cost us under $100. I would definitely recommend using an agent, as we did with Hotel Coral's driver, unless you have a really good knowledge of the language. Only one of the four people we interacted with spoke English.

> **TIP: If you speak fluent Spanish checking in at Customs and Immigration shouldn't be a problem. If you aren't fluent, consider hiring one of the many available agents in Ensenada. Ask other cruisers or the harbor master for recommendations.**

I spent the rest of the day doing laundry while Bryan finished the life-line netting. The boat had gotten pretty filthy over the last week, so before dinner we gave her a good scrubbing. Then we took our guidebooks and sat at the bar reviewing the charts and planning our course for the next few days. In the background, Monday night football was on the big screen, and although narrated in Spanish, it was a reminder that we still were not that far from home.

After studying the charts in greater detail, we decided to skip the anchorage at Colonet, a little more than 50 miles south of Ensenada. Instead, we opted to make a 24 hour passage straight to San Quintin. It would be our first overnight trip together, and Bryan asked me if I was nervous. I told him that I was not (which was true), but that staying awake for my watches might require large doses of caffeine. I also made him promise to wear his SOSpenders and tether at all times. To me, this issue was not negotiable. I hoped for a comfortable passage, and looked forward to what I would learn from the experience.

We were able to tune in the Baja Net on the Single Side Band the next morning, and were able to hear the weather report for the next few days. The report mentioned the possibility of rain and very little wind between Ensenada and San Quintin. Bryan asked me, "Well Honey, do you think you're up to it?" to which I replied that I was. I figured it probably wouldn't be any worse than the Catalina storm we got caught in a couple of weeks ago, and it could be a lot better. Partly I think I was just feeling anxious - anxious to get moving again, anxious to see what was out there, anxious to get further south where it might be warmer. I suppose I was a little anxious, too, because I didn't know what to expect. I had never made a passage that long, or overnight. I was curious about what the conditions would be like, both on the water and in the anchorages. I guess all the uncertainty made the goal-oriented, slightly neurotic part of my personality want to just charge full-speed ahead.

After getting fuel, we left Marina Coral at noon. As soon as we got outside the breakwater, it got a little bumpy, and there were ominous grey clouds on the horizon. The wind was right on our nose. It wasn't looking too good, and I think Bryan might have been a little concerned about subjecting me to such conditions on my first overnight trip. Sensing his trepidation, I said, "I think we should at least get around Punta Banda before we make any hasty decisions," and we agreed to continue on.

We had a school of dolphin escort us as we cleared the point and Isla Todos Santos a couple of hours later, and things settled down a bit. It was a little cool, but no rain. At the sighting of a huge mole (sunfish), Bryan joked "There's not much sun out here for you today, buddy." Around 5:30 PM, we had a spectacular sunset and took a bunch of pictures. We watched for the green flash, but it eluded us. For dinner I warmed up the homemade macaroni and cheese I had made the day before. I had been feeling pretty sleepy up to this point, but I guess nourishment was all I needed because I was awake enough to take the first watch. By 8:40 PM, Bryan and the dogs were sleeping in the cockpit, probably trying to keep me company. We listened to Jack Johnson and Donovan Frankenreiter on the IPOD. There was one other boat off our starboard side, but it was pretty far away. All in all, it was really was pretty peaceful.

From the log:

6:20 AM   Well, my first night watches are over. The sky is no longer black as pitch. I just checked on Bryan, asleep on the port side of the v-berth, crowded in between all the things I stowed on the starboard side and both dogs, who apparently felt they deserved to snuggle up to their dad on the big bed. They're all so zonked out, I figured I'd use this time to write this journal entry and give them a little longer to sleep.

My first watch, 8PM - 10PM, was pretty easy. I wrote, read, and monitored the radar and the fishing boats on our starboard side. Time passed quickly. The second watch, 12AM - 2AM, was a little less comfortable. It misted for the first 90 minutes, so I sat with my legs in the companionway and my back against the mizzen mast, reading my book by red light and trying to stay dry beneath the dodger. I hadn't slept much up to this point on my off-watches, so I was pretty tired by 2:00 AM. I was able to get a little sleep between 2AM and 4 AM before I had to get up and do it all over again. I read for awhile, fighting to keep my eyes open. Then dawn started breaking around 5:30, which helped me out tremendously. Isla San Martin is visible now off our port bow, about 20 miles away. I suppose I'll wake Bryan now and try to get in one more power nap before breakfast.

San Quintin and Passage
to Cedros Island

WE SPENT TWO NIGHTS IN the anchorage at San Quintin, 110 miles south of Ensenada. San Quintin is a huge bay, but the anchorage is nowhere near the little village, so while you are able to see buildings on the shore far in the distance, you cannot easily get to them.

We dropped our hook off the north-west point, in about 25 feet of water and about a half mile from shore. The beach was deserted, with a combination of lava rock formations near the water and windswept dunes a little higher up. This made for great tide pooling and exploring, giving us and the dogs ample opportunity to stretch our legs. There was a lot of marine life in San Quintin - dolphins, seals, and we even had a humpback whale surface about 10 feet from our dinghy one morning while taking the dogs to the beach.

> ### SAN QUINTIN
>
> *30° 21 N*
> *115° 58 W*
>
> <u>*Highlight*</u>: *Generally a calm overnight anchorage in NW winds. A nice beach with lava rock tide pools located on the west side of the bay.*
>
> *Note: There are no services easily accessible here.*

We felt rested up by Saturday morning, and decided to make the 130 mile passage to Cedros Island. We left San Quintin at 9:30 AM and were having a fairly comfortable sail until about 4:00 PM, when the winds and seas really started picking up. The next 16 hours were pretty hellish- huge, rolly following seas that made it impossible for the autopilot to keep up, leaving us to hand steer the entire time. Even though we weren't taking much spray over the bow, it was still pretty damp and cold. Bryan and I were both wearing harnesses and tethers while in the cockpit. At one point, after hearing a deafening noise while trying to get some rest inside the cabin, Bryan came rushing up through the companionway and excitedly said to me, "What happened?! What was that noise?" Noises are typically louder inside the boat than out, and because I had been outside with the noise of the wind and waves, I hadn't heard the noise as well as he had. In the dark and clipped in, he decided to go on deck and check it out because he thought the boom might have broken. Thankfully it hadn't. We were having issues with the dogs, also tethered in, but who were scared and anxious, and unable to find a comfortable spot to lay down where they wouldn't slide around. It was near impossible to sleep during our off-watches, so Bryan and I were exhausted. But we were also freezing cold, so on our off-watches we would go inside and try to warm up. On my watch, when I was in the cockpit alone, in the dark, with the wind ripping and the seas up around the combing when we were down in the trough of a wave, I was scared. Really scared. Really uncomfortable. Really cold. And thoroughly exhausted from gripping the wheel with all my might just to try to stay on course.

At one point in the early morning hours, I crawled into the v-berth to try and rest, only to discover that Sadie, who had been terrified and uncomfortable for the last 24 hours, had peed on our bed. I was so tired and my fuse was so short at that point that I was actually on the verge of tears. I knew we didn't have anymore clean sheets, not to mention my dilemma with trying to figure out where to stow stinky, peed-on sheets until I could wash them, which could be weeks. (In hindsight, I guess the worst case scenario would have been to wash them in the sink and hang them all over the boat to dry!) My log entry from 5:30 AM reads: *"What a miserable night. The seas made it very rolly and uncomfortable from about 5:00 PM on. Nobody got any rest. Sadie is miserable - cold, wet, and tired."* All in all, I was thinking that I might not have what it takes to endure too many passages like that one.

You can imagine then how much our spirits were lifted when the sun finally rose the next morning and we could see Cedros Island off our starboard bow. There are three anchorages on the leeward side of the island that are recommended in the guidebooks, and by 8:00 AM we had checked out the northernmost one. Our impression was that it wasn't much of an anchorage, so we headed south to the next one. It seemed a bit better, although not very protected, but we dropped anchor anyway. It only took us about ten minutes to decide the anchorage was too rolly and too overrun by kelp flies, aggressively swarming us and the dogs. We weighed anchor to head south again. The winds were calm by now and the sun was really warm, giving Bryan and I renewed energy, although in reality probably just masking the underlying exhaustion we were both fighting. When we pulled up to the third and southernmost anchorage on Cedros, we were disappointed to discover that not only was it very small and unprotected, the only real spot to anchor was already taken up by a large Mexican fishing boat.

We had to make a decision about what to do. Bryan said, "I'm feeling pretty good. I think we should take advantage of the nice weather to continue on to Turtle Bay." Turtle Bay was another 27 miles (and 6 hours!) away, but I, too, was feeling okay and concurred with Captain Bryan. This would put us in Turtle Bay around dusk, which we figured was early enough to get the anchor set and take our poor dogs and their bursting bladders to shore. As it turned out, we pulled in around 6:00 PM, having followed another sailboat in, and anchored in the dark. Our night vision was so screwed up- either from being so sleep deprived or from the huge mega yacht in the anchorage with every light onboard blazing- we couldn't tell which lights closer to the beach were from houses, the pier, or other boats. As a result of our confusion, we decided to play it safe for the night, anchoring a ways out in about thirty feet of water. (The light of the following morning revealed to us that we had actually anchored about four football fields away from the pier!) We spot cleaned the dirty sheets and put them in a trash bag for stowing, and dug out our sleeping bags. Sleep came easily that night in the calm, protected waters of Turtle Bay, a refuge from the elements we had endured for the past 33 hours. After all of our cruising time in Mexico, the passage from San Quintin to Turtle Bay is still remembered as one of our worst.

TIP: November and December temperatures on the outside of the Baja are cold, especially at night. Good quality foul weather gear, warm and water-resistant shoes, a wool beanie, and gloves are a must.

Turtle Bay –
New Friends and Mechanical Difficulties

WE WERE AWOKEN THE NEXT morning at 6:30 AM by someone knocking on the side of our hull and loudly trying to get our attention in Spanish. Apparently Captain Bryan wasn't the least bit concerned about who it may be or if they presented a threat of some kind because he was quick to inform me that I should be the one who went to see who it was. After all, he argued, my Spanish was so much better than his, and I would have a much easier time communicating with the mystery man, even if I *was* still in my pajamas!

TURTLE BAY

27° 38.5 N
114° 54 W

<u>Population</u>: *Approx. 1,000*

<u>Highlight</u>: *Located about halfway down the Baja peninsula and generally a calm all-weather anchorage. Fuel and limited provisions can be purchased here.*

Note: There are no bank or laundry facilities in Turtle Bay.

I finally managed to get the boards out of the companionway and scramble out, bed head and all. I was enthusiastically greeted by our visitor, a local guy floating next to our boat in a kayak, who explained that his name was Miquel and he comes around to collect trash from the boaters for a small fee. In the best Spanish I could manage at that hour, I teased him about how early it was. "It's only 6:30 in the morning," I exclaimed. Miquel responded with great amusement, educating me that the time was in fact 7:30, not 6:30. Apparently we had crossed into a new time zone without realizing. After my little tutorial, he also explained that he could get laundry done for us since there wasn't a laundromat where we could do it ourselves. We accepted his help for both services. Before he left, he joked with me (in Spanish, of course), that we had anchored really far out and that we should move the boat closer to town. He especially wanted us to move the boat closer before he had to paddle our clean laundry out to us the next day!

The rest of the morning was spent moving the boat and taking the dogs for a much needed walk. After our chores were done, we were ready for lunch and decided to try out the little restaurant overlooking the water. It was a warm, sunny afternoon, and we ended up sitting outside on the patio across from another American couple who seemed to be about our age. It would have been hard to miss them... the guy was about 6'5" with blond hair and fair skin, and the gal was about 5' with olive skin and dark hair, well-endowed, and scantily dressed. Considering where we were, they sort of stood out in the crowd. We all got to talking, and it turned out that Rob and Katrina were from Long Beach (near San Pedro), and they also owned a ketch (ketch owners seem to have a mutual admiration for one another). We visited for awhile and decided we should get together later for happy hour. We rendezvoused at sunset on Rob and Katrina's boat, the "S/v Blackwood," a Mariner 40 ketch, had snacks and drinks and visited awhile. We were pleased to discover that they are a very nice couple who were very easy to talk to, and they had an open itinerary for heading south, just as we did. We ended up spending a good deal of time with them the next day, as well, together indulging in a few $1.00 cervezas on the beach, where charismatic Rob with his habit of contributing to the local economy through his beer purchases, temporarily became the unofficial gringo mayor of Turtle Bay. The locals loved him so much the rest of us were a little worried he may never leave!

Wednesday turned out to be sort of a bummer day. When we had reanchored the boat on Monday, Bryan felt there wasn't as much water spitting out of the transom as there should be when the engine is running. Because we were planning to leave in a couple of days to buddy boat south with Katrina and Rob, he decided to check both the heat exchanger and the impeller. The heat exchanger was fine, but the raw water pump for the impeller was not - the keyway had broken. Not being very mechanical, Bryan had to explain to me that this is a BIG deal. We would need a whole new pump (which, of course, we didn't have a spare of), and it was most likely NOT something we could find in Turtle Bay. Basically, we were screwed. Being the impatient worrier that I am, I instantly began thinking we'd never make it south of Turtle Bay. I had visions of being stranded there forever. Fortunately, however, Bryan and Rob are much more optimistic, and put their creative minds to work on a solution. Rob and Katrina decided to contact their friend Tory on the VHF, who ironically had just left Turtle Bay on a delivery boat to San Diego, and would be driving back through Baja to his home in La Paz in a week or so. Tory, who we decided must be an angel, said it would be "no problem" to look for a replacement part for us in San Diego and then deliver it to us in Turtle Bay (which we figured would be about 200 miles out of his way). We exchanged emails and promised to send him all the serial numbers, etc that he would need to track down our part. In the meantime, our awesome new friends Katrina and Rob decided, without any hesitation, that they would wait with us in Turtle Bay until the boat got fixed so we could all head south together. That way, they said, they would be able to assist us with the repairs. Awfully generous for two people we had only met 48 hours earlier.

> **Tip: Always carry spare parts! If you have the spare, you improve your chances of attracting good luck and keeping things from breaking.**

We were still in Turtle Bay a week later, still with a broken boat, awaiting an email from Tory about whether or not he was able to find our part. That week was pretty nerve-wracking for us because of strong Santa Ana winds that blew relentlessly. If we were to drag anchor, Bryan and I had no engine to help get us out of what could have been a precarious situation. The good news was that we met someone in those few days who was eventually able to help us with our broken part. Upon hearing of our problem, Miguel (the local kayak guy), introduced us to his friend Alberto, who is a welder by trade. Attempting to converse in half Spanish, half English, Alberto agreed with us that what we really needed is a whole new pump, but in the absence of such, he offered to see what he could do for us as a temporary fix. I told him that in English we have a saying that would translate in Spanish to "es mejor de nada" (it's better than nothing), to which he chuckled and agreed.

A few nights later the winds finally died down enough for Bryan and me to get some quality sleep. The next day dawned sunny and warm, the winds actually didn't blow all day, and we started to feel really antsy to get our repairs done and head south. Bryan went to town to procure a piece of wood to use as a temporary mount for the solar panel we had decided to buy from Rob and Kat. We hoped it would produce enough amperage to allow us to invert whenever we want, as well as keep the batteries topped off so we wouldn't need to run the generator everyday. He also picked up our pump from Alberto, who did a really good weld job and only required $45 dollars and a six-pack as payment. This experience with "Alberto The Auto Mechanic" from Turtle Bay would prove to be one of our favorite stories to tell as the trip progressed.

> TIP: There is an expectation in remote parts of Baja that gringos come bearing gifts. Come prepared with t-shirts, candy, and school supplies to give away either in exchange for services rendered or simply as an expression of goodwill.

Turtle Bay-Abreojos-
Bahia Santa Maria

W E LEFT TURTLE BAY THE next morning at 9:00 AM. There was some weather headed down the Baja, said to be arriving in the Turtle Bay region Saturday or Sunday, and we wanted to get south of it.

We limped along at 4 knots, trying to go easy on our pump and the temporary fix Bryan and Alberto were able to rig. There wasn't much wind, unfortunately, but the seas were flat, and that was good for our nerves and for our dogs' peace of mind. There were eight sailboats transiting that day, including us and "S/v Blackwood." A boat behind us, "Veleda," was fortunate enough to catch a tuna, but we didn't catch anything other than bonita.

Rob and Katrina, and Bryan and I, were all very anxious to get out of Turtle Bay. We had been there for nine days, and they had been there for 15 days. It started to lose its charm around day four, when the Santa Ana's started blowing, and then continued to blow for the next five days. Everything on the boat was dirty from the excess of sand blowing off the beach. It was hard to sleep for the noise of the wind, whining through the rigging, and the fibers of the anchor rode stretching with each new gust, causing us to worry that the anchor might not hold.

The beaches in Turtle Bay are fairly dirty and the water smells pretty fishy - so much so that it fouled up our water maker filter and we were limited with the amount of water we could consume. This yucky water, combined with the chop caused by the wind, made taking the dogs to the beach a little less than pleasurable. On one particular afternoon, in trying to pick a spot of beach that was cleaner than the rest, if not a little rocky, I ended up a bloody mess and Sadie learned she could fly. In botched attempt at getting the dinghy off the beach through the swells, I lost my footing and fell onto a jagged piece of rock, cutting my knee open. When the swell picked up the bow of the dinghy, Sadie got launched backwards, past where Bryan was at the back of the boat, and ended up in the water. Paddling furiously and with eyes as big as saucers, I was just sure that if Sadie could talk, she would have told me she wasn't having very much fun on our little adventure to Mexico.

So were all a bit antsy to get out of there. It is really frustrating when you have no control over the situation affecting you and your boat. We couldn't do anything to fix the problem without parts available, so thank goodness we met Alberto. Tory wouldn't have been able to deliver the part we needed until Friday or so, which was just too close to the bad weather for our comfort. Not to sound redundant, but we all were ready to hit the road. We had thought about spending some time on Thursday in Abreojos, maybe long enough to have Thanksgiving dinner with Rob and Kat. Really, though, all we really wanted was to get to Bahia Santa Maria (Mag Bay) by Friday night.

Our passage from Turtle Bay to Abreojos was a dream. It was 24 hours of warmth and flat, calm seas. There were eight sailboats making the passage from Turtle Bay, so we had lots of company. We caught lots of fish (11 in total), but they were all mackerel and bonito, and not the type of fish we like to eat. We pulled into Abreojos around 9:30 AM, and there weren't any other boats there. We dropped our hook, as did Rob and Kat, and quickly figured out why there weren't any other boats there. It was a very rolly anchorage. Still, we wanted to take the dogs to shore, so we lowered the dinghy into the water.

Our dinghy landing was a bit exciting, as a reef fringes the left side of the beach and there were big breakers on the right side. Worried that this was not going to go well, I tried to convince Bryan that the dogs could go to the bathroom on the deck so we wouldn't have to beach it, to no avail. Needless to say, we landed without too much drama and the dogs were very grateful. Our departure from the beach, however, was a whole different story. We thought we had timed it right, but alas, we took two big waves right over front of the dinghy and almost lost little Sadie (again). From her spot in the bow of the dinghy, she literally flew up in the air and backwards when we were clobbered by one of the waves, and landed in the water behind the outboard engine. We were all soaked. I had to bail water out of the dinghy all the way back to the boat! I'm sure we were the day's entertainment for the panga fisherman on the beach, who must have been calling us loco gringo marineros.

Upon hearing of our debacle, Kat and Rob decided they didn't really need to go to shore. Instead, we decided to hoist our anchors and head to Bahia Santa Maria. We were all pretty exhausted from our overnighter and knew that the next leg would be a long one, but Abreojos was too rolly for any of us to get any rest. Out of Abreojos, we were able to get in some sailing. But about sundown, the rolly, following seas found us yet again and things started getting uncomfortable. Not only did the dogs hate those kinds of conditions, but our autopilot would act up, and we would end up hand-steering for hours at a time. Not a big deal on a short passage, but a HUGE deal on an overnighter. It was Thanksgiving Day, so I wanted to prepare something nice and warm for dinner. I managed to make beef with rice and corn, all the while wedging myself into the galley and trying to keep the pots from going airborne with every pitch and roll. From the cockpit, Bryan would call out to me "SWELL!" and I would lift the pot of boiling water off the stove with one hand and hold on to the pot of beef with the other. Not really so much fun.

Neither one of us got any quality sleep that night, so by Friday we were truly wiped out. We got into Bahia Santa Maria around 5PM. There were already five other boats on anchor, some of whom we recognized from Turtle Bay. It was pretty breezy, but flat. No swell. Thank goodness. We could make out that Bahia Santa Maria is a very large bay and is shaped somewhat like the letter "C" if it were facing backwards. This provides good protection from the wind and swell that come out of the west and north in the fall and winter months.

We got the anchor set, and then in that deceiving light that happens just before dark, took the dogs to shore. The beach in Santa Maria is shallow a long way out (especially at low tide). When we landed the dinghy in last few minutes of the dusky early evening light, we were tricked into thinking we were actually at the beach, only to discover we were really still a long, long way from it. We pulled the dinghy toward the beach for the longest time without ever finding dry sand. The dogs were so desperate that they jumped out of the dinghy and ended up doing their business in about four inches of water! We had never seen them do that before. Desperate times call for desperate measures! With our grateful dogs we headed back and cleaned up the boat, took showers, and had something to eat. We were exhausted. Those overnighters really zap you if you can't get any sleep on your off-watch. Thank goodness Bahia Santa Maria was calm that day, because we were able to get a great night's sleep.

Bahia Santa Maria
and our Thanksgiving Dinner

WE SPENT FOUR NIGHTS IN Bahia Santa Maria, and all-in-all, it was a great anchorage and we had a really nice time there. Except for a few beach huts belonging to local panga fishermen, Santa Maria is uninhabited. The beach, made up of over seven miles of unspoiled, shell-covered sand, windswept dunes, and a fringe of mangroves, is clean and beautiful - a welcome

BAHIA SANTA MARIA

24° 44.4 N
112° 15 W

<u>Highlight</u>: *An excellent anchorage with good protection in NW weather. Miles of unspoiled, shell-covered beaches.*

Note: No services available.

site after the dirty, litter-strewn beaches we had encountered further north. There are literally millions of shells on the beach in Santa Maria- sand dollars, huge clam shells of various colors, coffee beans, spirals, and so forth. There are so many shells that Bryan and I kept remarking that my mom would go nuts in this place, and that Dad would have to buy a bigger boat just to take all the shells home that she would collect. I will admit that I saved a few of the ones I found, but no more than what would fit in a Ziploc bag.

We spent a lot of time with Kat and Rob in Santa Maria, walking the beach and sharing meals. Because we had been in transit on Thanksgiving Day, we had decided to have our holiday dinner together on Saturday. I made green beans with bacon and onion, homemade bread, and pumpkin pie. Kat and Rob provided the appetizers and surprised us with a wonderful jumbalaya dish made with fresh lobster they bought from the panga fishermen that morning. Dinner was excellent, and we were all stuffed at the end of the night. We talked about how great turkey and all the fixings sounded, but agreed that our dinner was more than acceptable.

We were lucky enough to make some new friends in Santa Maria. CiCi and Christy from s/v Island Girl were at anchor for the same days we were. Christy, the owner of the 31' Pearson, was on her way to Puerto Vallarta, and her friend CiCi was crewing for her. CiCi looked familiar to Bryan and me, and we thought we recognized her as a shoreboat driver from Two Harbors. It turns out we were right! What a small world. We talked about all the people and places we all are familiar with, and even discovered that she knows my parents from all the time they spend at the island.

On our last night in Bahia Santa Maria, Kat and Rob invited everyone to their boat for happy hour. Everyone provided something to eat and/or drink, and I was left thinking how amazing it is that we cruisers, anchored in the remote corners of Baja, can be so fortunate as to dine on chicken pesto sausage, brie and crackers, champagne, wine, and good rum. In many ways we are definitely "roughing it" out here, but you would never know it by the spread we put out at happy hour! Life is good!

> TIP: Take advantage of Bahia Santa Maria's fabulous expanse of beach to get some exercise, and collect some sand dollars while you're at.

Adventures in Magdalena Bay and Passage to Cabo San Lucas

After our stay in Bahia Santa Maria, we moved to Man 'O War cove, inside Magdalena Bay. As the crow flies, the distance from Santa Maria to Man 'O War is not more than 10 miles, but because you have to go around Punta Entrada to the south to get there, the trip ends up taking about 8 hours. Because we were waiting for a weather window to head to Cabo San Lucas, we had decided to move over to Man 'O War cove where it was rumored we could provision, get fuel, and

> **MAN O' WAR COVE**
> **(Magdalena Bay)**
>
> *24° 38.09 N*
> *112° 80.13 W*
>
> <u>Population</u>: *Less than 100*
>
> <u>Highlight</u>: *A good place to ride out bad weather. Diesel can be delivered by panga if needed; limited provisions and internet service can be obtained in the main town of San Carlos, 30 minutes away by panga.*

have access to an internet cafe. What we discovered when we arrived is that although there are about 40 houses there, Man 'O War cove is very remote and offers no services. The port captain, however, is able to acquire fuel for boaters, which he then delivers himself. Knowing that most sailboaters don't want to take their boats any further up the lagoon because of the shoals, he also offers panga rides to San Carlos (about 30 minutes away) for $10 per person so that cruisers can go to the market, the internet café, and the hardware store.

TIP: It is smart to always use a "Baja filter" when taking on fuel in the remote parts of Mexico. Get one at Downwind Marine in San Diego before heading south.

Because we all needed groceries and were anxious to email our families, we decided to make the trip to San Carlos. Excited about my outing to the "big city," I decided to dress a little nicer than usual, and put on clean shorts and a clean shirt, and dug my "nice" sandals (the dressiest of my flip flop selection) out of the locker. I don't know what I was expecting exactly, but I wasn't expecting what we got! Bryan and I, Rob and Kat, and Ian and Lynn from s/v Cloud Nine were picked up at 8AM and chauffeured to town in a rugged wooden skiff with seats damp from the morning condensation. Thinking we would be dropped off at a pier or a dock of some sort, we were a bit surprised when our captain pulled into shallow water at the beach, thick with neon green moss, and parked the bow of the panga on the slimy mud. To exit the skiff, we had to scramble over the bow and hop down about three feet, trying not to lose our footing and end up in the sludge. Luckily, none of us ended up on our rears.

Since we hadn't been deposited anywhere close to the center of town, I asked the captain for directions to the market and internet cafe. He made a vague, sweeping arc motion with his arm, and said everything was "in the center" of town. Hmm... So we set off walking, over the sand and down a dirt road, past a house with two barking dogs on the roof (yes, on the roof!), passing in front of a school with broken down pangas in the yard. Eventually, we wound up at a market that seemed to have some promise, so I asked the clerk if she knew where the internet cafe was. She happily told me that it was right across the street. Apparently, we had walked right by it. This is easy to do, however, because we have discovered that most of the internet cafes on the Pacific side of Baja look nothing like the internet cafes we are familiar with back home. Usually, the Baja version is merely an otherwise vacant building with concrete floors, bad lighting, and no sign out front. Upon entering, you generally find a few computers with really slow dial-up connections set up on plastic lawn furniture. Thankfully, the cost is usually no more than $1.50 per hour. It's nice to be able to email family and let them know we're okay, but sometimes I really miss high-speed wi-fi.

After shooting off an email to the folks back home, we had some tacos with Rob and Kat at an outdoor stand, and then went to the market. Shopping was becoming a bit of a sport for all of us, because it seems we always had at least a 15 minute walk back to the dinghy (or in this case, the panga), and then at least another ten minute ride back to the boat. This can be a challenge when you have to carry groceries, water, beer, ice and whatever else we feel we can't live without. On this particular day in San Carlos, with our arms loaded down with heavy bags of groceries, beer, and ice, we were feeling a bit overwhelmed by the task facing us, and opted instead to cram into a taxi. A worthwhile expenditure of $6.00, for sure! At the time it didn't really dawn on us that it was odd for such a small town to have a fleet of taxis. San Carlos doesn't even have a bank, but they have taxis!

Back at the boat, the rest of the day was fairly routine. We took the dogs to the beach, tried to find clams in the damp sand of low tide (with no success), and finished the night off on the S/v Blackwood, where Kat prepared dinner for all of us. The next day we woke to the alarm clock at 6:30 AM, and began our preparations for a 7:30 departure. By 7:45 we had raised the anchor and were on course for Cabo San Lucas, our last leg of the Baja peninsula. While it is true what they say about the Pacific side of the Baja being wonderfully remote and rugged, undeveloped and unspoiled, I think we were all anxious for our landfall in Cabo and some time in civilization as we know it. We needed to do laundry, call our families, and pick up some marine supplies. It would be nice to visit a bank, grab a meal in a restaurant, and maybe buy a newspaper. Cabo was said to be very expensive- $165 a night for a 45' slip - so we knew we probably would not stay long. Still, it would most likely be a much appreciated port of call.

From the log:

Our passage today has been enjoyable. It's almost 11:00 PM and I'm on watch. We had a gorgeous, warm day with mild winds and seas. Kat and Rob have been just off our bow all day. We caught a few fish, but nothing edible, so they all were thrown back. It was so calm I even managed to give Sadie a bath and a haircut on the deck this afternoon. After making teriyaki chicken bowls for dinner, Bryan and I set up the laptop in the cockpit and watched a movie. We've passed two cruise ships and a sailboat, all heading north. There is no moon tonight, so you can see millions of stars in the night sky. We're making decent time, so by my estimation we should arrive in Cabo around 6:00 PM tomorrow.

Cabo San Lucas

WE HAD A GREAT TRIP from Magdalena Bay to Cabo San Lucas –the boat ran great, we had calm seas and warm weather. We were finally able to wear bathing suits. We approached the north end of Cabo Falso, about 15 miles north of Cabo San Lucas, around 1:00 PM today. For the next three hours, we followed its white sand-dune covered coastline for what seemed like forever. We could finally make out Cabo's famous arches at Lover's Beach around 4:00 PM.

> ### CABO SAN LUCAS
>
> *22° 53 N*
> *109° 53 W*
>
> <u>Population</u>: +/- 50,000
>
> <u>Highlight</u>: *The first port south of Ensenada where all services can be obtained- groceries, laundry, banks, marine repairs, and postal service. Restaurants, movie theatres, as well as a full-service (although expensive) marina located here, also.*

Excited and overwhelmed by a surge of accomplishment, we hailed S/v Blackwood on the radio and suggested we all have a celebratory cocktail as we rounded the point. They agreed, of course, and we got some great pictures of each other as the two boats sailed side by side. To make the moment even more amazing, we were joined for about 30 minutes by a whale that swam between us and S/v Blackwood, as if escorting us to Land's End.

As soon as we approached Land's End, we were bombarded by boat traffic - a cruise ship, charter boats, waverunners, and para-sailers- a bit jarring to the psyche after three weeks of traveling the outside of the Baja. Having already decided we wouldn't go into the marina for a slip, we anchored off the beach in front of all the big hotels. When we took the dogs to shore, we immediately noticed that the water was considerably warmer here. The beach was fairly steep, making it a little challenging to beach the dinghy, but it was nonetheless beautiful. Tourists rode horses up and down the beach on sand that was a muted shade of pink, and families played in the surf with their children. In the distance, music could be heard coming from the beachfront bars. It was good to be here, even if for just a short while.

> TIP: For the average cruiser, Cabo is priced out. Use this stop solely for reprovisioning, a visit to the bank, and a chance to do laundry... and then move on.

Chapter 4

Cabo San Lucas to La Paz
An Exercise in Patience

Stuck in Los Frailles

WE STAYED IN CABO FOR five days, and while I enjoyed our time there, it was time to leave. It is easy to spend too much money there, just as I imagined it would be easy to get way too comfortable, with restaurants, internet cafes, grocery stores, laundromats, and so on. So we left on the morning of December 7th for the anchorage at Los Frailles, 43 miles to the north. Getting out of the marina proved to be quite a challenge, as we opted to leave at 6AM, which as luck would have it, is the same time all of Cabo's hundred or so sportfishers head out for a day of fishing. We had to stop at the fuel dock on our way out, which meant Bryan had to skillfully maneuver the boat amongst all the power boats and bait pangas who seemed to have no regard for a lone sailboat in their midst. What an ordeal! But we pulled it off without getting creamed.

For about the first hour out of the harbor, it looked like we were going to have a nice sail. It was warm, there was only a slight bit of swell, and the wind was coming from just the right direction. However, after our fabulous passage from Mag Bay to Cabo, we should have known not to get too greedy. King Neptune did not allow the favorable conditions to last for long. Once we rounded Punta Palmilla, the wind built to 25 knots and the seas to 6-8 feet, both right on our nose. This was not what the weather report called for!

We were only able to do about 2.5 knots, sometimes less. We were talking to Rob and Kat on the VHF, and they were doing worse than us. The Blackwood is a full-keeled boat and therefore much heavier. They were only averaging about 1 knot. In complete frustration, Rob said to us over the VHF radio, "Dude, I swear, sometimes my knot meter is reading 0.00!" Those kinds of conditions put a lot of strain on the boat and on the crew, so we had a decision to make. We knew we couldn't afford to go back to Cabo and get a slip at the marina, and we didn't want to re-anchor off the beach if the swells were going to be big.

Rob called us on the radio again. "I've altered my heading to Mazatlan. The ride is much better. Maybe we should skip La Paz altogether." Bryan replied, "What's your heading?" Rob gave us his course, and we altered our heading, too. After a couple of minutes went by, Bryan studied the GPS/chart plotter. He called Rob back. "Rob, that's not the heading for Mazatlan. That's the heading for Puerto Vallarta." Either way, we decided both ports were still a great distance further than the anchorage that awaited us at Los Frailles. We opted to stick with the plan to spend a few days at Los Frailles, ultimately heading to La Paz for Christmas and New Year's. By the time we reached Los Frailles, it was 10:15 PM. What should have been an 8 hour day sail had turned into 15 hours of bashing north. Rob and Kat made it also, arriving an hour after us.

While for us it still wasn't as rough as our trip from San Quintin to Cedros Island, Rob felt it was the roughest passage they had made so far. The light of the next day revealed that he had indeed burned a great deal more fuel than usual. A lot of his rigging was loose and would need to be adjusted before we went north.

Los Frailles

THE ANCHORAGE AT LOS FRAILLES is at the north end of the bay, a fish camp is on the middle part of the beach, and a couple of houses and RV's take up seasonal residence south of that. The beach is very pretty and seems to go on forever to the south. Unlike the Pacific side, there is hardly any swell here, which makes landing the dinghy pretty easy. You can fish from the beach, snorkel the calm waters of the anchorage, or hike the hills on the north end of the bay. We spent our days leisurely, walking the dogs on the beach, talking with the campers, and playing bocce ball and volleyball with the other cruisers. It is easy to see why so many Canadians and Americans choose to spend their winters here; Bryan believes he will remember it as one of his favorite anchorages from both of his trips to Baja.

> **Los Frailles**
>
> 23° 23 N
> 109° 24 W
>
> *Highlight:*
> *Once a week, both the pastry truck and the produce truck make a stop here. Take advantage of this opportunity to buy donuts as well as fresh fruits and veggies.*

Although the anchorage was very nice and we found activities to pass the time, the next few days proved to be another exercise in patience. Everyday and every night the wind blew, and then blew some more. It kept all the boats here trapped inside the protection of the anchorage. The swells outside were 6 - 8 feet, and the wind was averaging 25 knots out of the northwest, which happened to be the way we needed to go.

All in all we ended up spending eight nights in Los Frailles. We were joined by some boats familiar to us from previous stops along the Baja – s/v Moorea, s/v Simplicity, s/v Alcyon, and s/v Socahtoa. We made the most of the time, snorkeling, playing beach volleyball and bocce ball, and having a few meals at the one restaurant in the area, about a half mile walk from the anchorage. We spent more time with Kelly and Kelly from s/v Moorea, having a potluck on their boat one night along with Rob and Kat, and playing cards another night. The night before we left to head north, we had them over to our boat for movie night, where we watched "Surviving Christmas" and shared popcorn and cookies. Kelly and Kelly, who have taken to calling themselves, "El Kelly" and "La Kelly" while in Mexico, are from Seattle and are planning to go at least as far as New Zealand, and maybe even circumnavigate. It was great fun getting to know them and spending time with yet another couple our age.

TIP: Your plans will often be delayed because of bad weather or unfavorable conditions. This is part of cruising, and the sooner you accept it, the more you will enjoy the whole experience. The happiest cruisers are patient cruisers!

From the log:

Today is Friday, December 16th and we are about 5 hours out of La Paz. We left Los Frailles last night at 5:00 PM when the winds laid down. Also leaving with us were S/v Blackwood, S/v Moorea, and S/v Simplicity. Although it was another overnighter, the passage so far has been quite comfortable. The afternoon winds are starting to build now, but we're still averaging 4.5 knots, and the seas are calm. It will be nice to get to La Paz and celebrate Christmas. It will also be a relief to fix all the things on our boat that now need fixing - the raw water pump, the windlass (which broke as we were leaving Cabo), the starter (which started acting up in Los Frailles), and the automatic bilge pump switch. Bryan also thinks he needs to tinker with the batteries and the refrigeration. Looks like we'll be in La Paz for awhile, but that's okay with us. We're hoping some friends and family will be able to visit.

Chapter 5

A Cruiser's Christmas
in La Paz

Arrival in La Paz / Christmas Cruiser-style

WE ARRIVED AT MARINA Costa Baja in La Paz around 4:30 PM on the 16th of December. It was such a great feeling to finally be there, knowing we could now start repairs on the boat and get ready for the Christmas holiday. We were checking in at the marina office at the same time as Terry from s/v SouthWind III, whom we had briefly met in Los Frailles, and we opted for slips next to each other. That night Terry invited us to his boat for a fabulous dinner of freshly-caught dorado. It was nice to know that some people were actually catching fish, even if we weren't! The next day we were joined on the dock by Tim from s/v Bogtrotter (another SoCal cruiser), as well as Rob and Kat. It was fun to have all four boats together for the next week. Everyone was busy working on boat projects, but we still found time to enjoy of couple of happy hours together.

La Paz
24° 13 N
110° 20 W
Population: 180,000
Highlight: La Paz is a haven for cruisers, boasting 3 marinas, 2 fuel docks, haul-out yards, chandleries, and repair shops. Additionally, a multitude of day trips can be made from here to nearby islands and anchorages.

Marina Costa Baja is very impressive. With a capacity for 300 boats ranging in size from 25 to 150 feet, the harbor is divided into two basins by a dredged channel. Separating the two basins is the Fiesta Inn, a large, modern hotel overlooking the marina and the beach, as well as a new condominium development. The inner basin is bordered on two sides by a collection of brand new upscale restaurants and shops, a market, and a miniature golf course. The marina boasts its own desalinization plant, a large fuel dock, and pumpouts at every slip (yes, every slip. You never have to move your boat when you need to pump out!) The entire complex is nicely landscaped with various types of cactus, bougainvillea, and palm trees. The buildings are painted orange and cream and constructed in an adobe style. Slip renters and condominium owners reap the benefits of 24 hour security, clean facilities, internet access, and a free shuttle service to town. Additionally, cruisers are granted free use of the hotel's amenities, namely a gym and three pools. While the marina was not at full capacity when we were there, we met several cruisers who had been here for many months (and some who had been in La Paz for a number of years) and claim that Marina Costa Baja is the best of the four marinas in La Paz.

Over our first few days in the marina, we got a handful of boat projects done, took advantage of the hotel's gym, and met some really nice other cruisers. We went downtown to the marine stores and hardware stores, as well as the grocery store. The biggest grocery store in town is called "CCC," and let me tell you, it was a real treat! It's huge and has a great selection of meats, dairy, produce, wines, and liquors. In addition, there is a deli and a coffee bar, a panaderia (bakery), and a tortillaria for fresh corn and flour tortillas. Along with the turkey we found, I found numerous brands that I would normally find in the States, and was excited to discover that I could make our Christmas meal really special.

On December 21st, Bryan and I met up with "El Kelly" and "La Kelly" in town. The guys had decided previously that they wanted to go Christmas shopping together, which left us girls to do the same. Everything in La Paz is centrally located near the "malecon," Mexico's equivalent of a waterfront boardwalk, making our Christmas shopping pretty convenient. I think we walked at least 80% of downtown that day, but in the end, found everything we were looking for, including a machete for Kelly's husband. I was surprised by the multitude of shops downtown, including two large department stores, a number of pharmacies, a Radio Shack, clothing and shoe stores, jewelry stores, furniture stores, traditional souvenir shops, and so on. The four of us finished the day off on one of the waterfront benches, resting our feet and enjoying an ice cream cone, and remarked to each other that you truly could find just about everything you could want or need in downtown La Paz.

On Friday the 23rd, Bryan got up early and caught the 9AM shuttle into town. He had been working on our roller-fuller and needed to find new bearings. When he was done around 12:30, he met up with "El Kelly" and "La Kelly" at the shuttle stop and brought them back to Marina Costa Baja for the grand tour. They have been anchored out near Marina de La Paz, about 4 miles away, and wanted to see all that our marina had to offer. We showed them around and then had lunch together at one of the marina's outdoor restaurants. In the afternoon, after saying good-bye to our friends, we moved our boat from our original slip in the outer basin to a new slip in the inner basin. We wanted to be a little closer to the facilities and more protected from the wind. Our new slip was on "I" dock, where we quickly met our new neighbors Pat and Rod, and their beagle-mix "Matey," aboard s/v Bagabundo, an Offshore 40.

The next day was Christmas Eve, and there were many preparations to be made. I started by baking brownies, moved on to banana bread, and finished with pumpkin pie. It was a beautiful and warm day, so after I felt I had been cooped up in the galley for long enough, Bryan and I went for a dinghy ride around the marina. We had to pinch ourselves that it was Christmas Eve and there we were in shorts and bare feet, enjoying 80 degree weather in Mexico. Later that evening we joined up with all our new cruiser friends in the marina's lounge for a Christmas potluck and an entertaining white elephant gift exchange. The evening culminated aboard s/v Bagabundo, where we shared wine and conversation with Rod and Pat.

Christmas morning started off with a bang when we let the dogs have the gifts from their stockings, namely bags of treats and new squeaky toys. Bryan and I then opened our stockings and our gifts. Bryan got new trunks, a Hawaiian shirt, a pocket knife and a CD holder; I got a pair of pants, a backpack, a woven basket for my produce, and two sarongs. We spent the rest of the day talking on the phone with family back home and getting ready for Christmas dinner. We made pumpkin bread, wheat beer bread, and applesauce. Kat and

Rob joined us for holiday dinner, and just like at Thanksgiving, we had a feast: turkey, stuffing, mashed potatoes and gravy, two kinds of bread, cranberry sauce, vegetables, and pumpkin pie. While we missed our family back home, it really was a nice Christmas.

> **TIP: Even though La Paz is home to an abundance of gringos, you should still do all you can to respect the local culture. Speak Spanish as much as you can and dress modestly.**

NEW YEAR'S, HOLIDAY BOWL GAMES, AND A FAMILY VISIT

After the festivities of Christmas, things were quiet around the marina for a few days. We actually got some sanding and varnishing done, although there was still another coat or two to be applied. Then New Year's Eve rolled around, which of course meant more parties, food, and even a fireworks show. We hung out in the cruiser's lounge at the marina, having cocktails and watching the ball drop in Times Square. It was the latest Bryan and I had stayed up in months (other than our watches, of course, which don't really count)!

Starting on January 2nd, we watched the college football bowl games in the cruiser's lounge with all our new friends. You could almost forget you were in Mexico, except for the announcers speaking in Spanish. Our football fix culminated on January 4th with the Rose Bowl, when we packed about 20 people into the lounge to watch the game. And what a great game it was! Mom and Dad were actually at the game, and of course were rooting for USC, as were most of the people watching the game with us, and were therefore sad to see them lose to Texas.

The next day my parents flew to La Paz for a week long visit. They spent their first night in Cabo San Lucas, which was especially enjoyable for Mom because she had never been there. The next day they drove up to La Paz, arriving in the mid afternoon. After checking in to the hotel, they joined Bryan and me, and our friend

Tim (s/v Bogtrotter), aboard Salty Dog, where we all sat around in the cockpit for a couple of hours having cocktails and shooting the breeze before proceeding to one of the restaurants in the marina for dinner. Saturday was spent touring the condos available for purchase at Marina Costa Baja and poking around down at Marina de La Paz for the monthly cruiser's swap meet. We took Mom and Dad to the CCC grocery store so they could see for themselves how big and well-stocked it is, and bought groceries for the next day's outing.

On Sunday we took the boat to Balandra Bay, about an hour and a half away. Balandra is absolutely beautiful, with white sand beaches and water that goes from the palest blue to the deepest turquoise. After anchoring the boat, we took a dinghy ride past popular Mushroom Rock and explored the beaches for shells for about an hour. Back on the boat, we barbequed cheeseburgers and relaxed. When the wind picked up, we decided to head back to the marina. Dad sailed the boat most of the way, the whole time marveling at Mexico's warm January weather.

Monday proved to be another busy day of sightseeing. We started off the morning at Gorilla Grill, one of our favorite breakfast spots in La Paz, and then ventured to the big shopping complex uptown that houses a City Club (like Costco), a gigantic Soriano's grocery store, a Dorian's department store, and a movie theatre. From here we headed back downtown to walk the streets near the malecon and explore La Paz's souvenir shops. About mid-afternoon we piled back into the rental car, picked up the dogs from the boat, and drove out to Tecolote Beach, on the northern tip of the peninsula. It was a bit windy, but we still enjoyed margaritas at Palapa Azul while looking out at Isla Espiritu Santo.

Tuesday was our day to set out for Buena Vista, a two hour car ride south of La Paz and an important destination for us because it is Victorville's sister city. After Dad's breakfast of coffee and tamales from one of the restaurants in the marina, we headed south around 11:00 AM. Our first stop was at La Ventana, a spot famous for windsurfing and kite boarding about 45 minutes from La Paz. There were probably thirty or forty kites out on the water that day, making for a beautiful scene. From here, we headed south again to Los Muertos, one of the more popular anchorages in the Sea of Cortez. (Its location makes it the shortest point from which to cross to the mainland.) We had lunch there at the Giggling Marlin, and although we had great food, Bryan was disappointed to see a commercial venture like the Giggling Marlin staking a claim to a previously desolate and remote anchorage known primarily to sailors and fisherman. His disappointment was compounded by a gigantic resort and housing development underway in Los Muertos as well, a development that wasn't there a year and a half ago on his first trip to the area. While modern day development in beautiful places like this is inevitable, it is nevertheless sad to us sailors who were previously the only ones privileged to enjoy these remote places undisturbed by man.

We left Los Muertos and headed across a 15 mile dirt road back to the main highway, much to Bryan's amusement (he was reliving his off-roading days) and Mom's displeasure (due to her bad back). Highway 1 then wound through the Sierra de la Laguna mountain range for about an hour before dropping us back down to East Cape, and eventually the sleepy beach town of Buena Vista. Finding the hotel was a bit of a challenge, due to its lack of signage and the absence of street signs for the multitude of dirt roads, but we eventually arrived around 3:30 PM. We checked into our nice bungalow-style rooms and toured the property, ending up at the bar for a couple of margaritas. The Hotel Spa Buena Vista is even nicer than I remember from my first trip here in 1990. The pools are fabulous; I could see myself lounging there for hours if our visit was longer. Everybody was pretty wiped out after dinner, so we turned in early. Mom and Dad got up early the next morning and walked the beach on both sides of the resort, marveling at all the beautiful homes and the number of gringos living in them. In fact, they even ran into someone with a connection to Victorville and chatted with them for a while. Sadly, we had to leave soon after breakfast because Dad and Mom had to catch a flight out of San Jose del Cabo. Bryan and I were so happy to share a week with them, but for me, it was really hard to say good-bye to them again. Being apart from family was one of the hardest parts of the trip.

From the log:

Since Mom and Dad left, things have been pretty mellow around here. Bryan and I spent a few days sanding and varnishing (a task that seems to forever be on the to-do list) and had the raw water pump and the starter rebuilt. Our friend Tim on s/v Bogtrotter was getting ready to leave for Mazatlan and then on to Costa Rica, so a bunch of us got together on his boat one night for a carne asada feast. The next day Bryan and Tim decided to go fishing in the dinghy, so I tagged along. No one caught anything, but that's no real surprise.

Soon after Mom and Dad's departure, our friends "El Kelly" and "La Kelly" on s/v Moorea arrived at Marina Costa Baja, much to our delight. We hadn't seen them for about three weeks, since they left after Christmas to spend some time up north in the anchorages of the Sea of Cortez. They spent four nights in the marina and had the slip right next to us. On Sunday, a Super Bowl BBQ had been organized at the bar in the marina by Jeff on s/v Moon Me (yes, his boat's name is Moon Me!). Again, we had loads of food. And being from Seattle, Kelly and Kelly were thrilled with the Seahawk's victory. On Monday, "El Kelly" taught Bryan how to give me a haircut... I really, really needed it, but needless to say, I was a bit nervous about the boys cutting my hair. Thankfully, they did a fabulous job. And what an event! Bryan then conceded to let me trim his goatee, and if you know him at all, you know that's a major big deal! We even managed to have a pizza night before Kelly and Kelly's departure from Costa Baja. "La Kelly" taught me how to make home-made pizza dough, and we had four different kinds of pizza for dinner, some baked in the oven and some done on the grill. Pizza on the BBQ... what won't we cruisers do when we need a fix?!

CALIFORNIA TRIP

By the second week of February, after spending a couple of weeks engrossed in boat projects, Spanish classes, the NFL playoffs, and Super Bowl parties, Bryan and I decided to make a quick trip home to California. We knew we would have to make the trip sometime soon to renew our tourist visas (as we had been advised that the Mexican government won't let you do so without leaving the country for at least 24 hours), so we decided to spend five days at home, visiting family and friends.

While it was a short trip - only four nights - we had a great time in CA. We were able to see many friends, all of whom we've missed greatly while we've been gone. We returned to La Paz on Friday night, and were able to pick up the dogs from the kennel on Saturday morning. We had missed them so much, and judging by their greeting, the feeling was mutual. The site of our filthy, stinky dogs confirmed that kennel care in Mexico (or at least in La Paz) is not of the same quality you get in the States. We would decide to avoid boarding them again at all costs. Lesson learned, you could say.

From the log:

Now that we're back, we are preparing to leave on the 17th or 18th for Mazatlan. It's about time! We've been in La Paz for two months, and while it will be sad to say good-bye to all the great friends we have made here, it's time to move on. Bryan says he knows it's time to go because he can now get around downtown without having to look at a map or street signs!

Our first stop will be in Los Muertos, a 10 hour sail south of here. We'll spend the night and leave for Mazatlan the next day, a 195 mile trip across the Sea of Cortez that will take us two full days. Mazatlan will be our first stop in a place more tropical than what we've experienced so far, and we are anxiously looking forward to the next leg of our adventure.

Saturday, February 16th: We're still in La Paz. Still at Marina Costa Baja. We're waiting for a better weather window to head to Muertos, then on to Mazatlan. It's nice here in La Paz, warm with only mild breezes but the SSB is reporting winds in the 20-25 knot range in the part of the Sea where we need to be. In our boat, that's just a bit too much wind for us and the dogs to be comfortable.

Our staying in La Paz was beneficial to us in two ways, however. First off, we ended up having to take Sadie to the vet because we discovered while walking her one morning that she had blood in her urine. Had we left on Thursday like we planned, we would have been at least four days from a vet. As it turns out, we were able to take Sadie to Dr. Tomas, a highly recommended vet here in La Paz who speaks English. After examining her, he diagnosed her with kidney stones. She was given two shots- an antibiotic and an anti-inflammatory - and we got out of there for the whopping price of $18. That visit would have cost us at least 3 digits in the U.S. Additionally, he sent us to the pharmacy to pick up two prescriptions and some Vitamin C for her, which cost us a mere $20.

The second reason we're glad we stayed a bit longer in La Paz was because we were able to attend a party given for our friend Jeff on s/v Moon Me. Jeff and his boat had become notorious in this part of Mexico, and the party was given in honor of him selling Moon Me after many years of adventure and craziness. The party was hosted by the people who purchased the boat - Fred and Redmond, who are a little crazy also- and had a theme reminiscent of the old TV show "This Is Your Life." Many of the marina locals participated in the skit that turned out to be hilarious and entertaining, and left Jeff speechless and most likely a little embarrassed, especially when the crowd had the opportunity to get even with him with a group moon. Good, clean fun was had by all, and I really couldn't remember the last time I laughed so much.

Chapter 6

Mazatlan-Isla Isabela-
Puerto Vallarta
A Month On The Mainland

Mazatlan

WE ENDED UP SPENDING THREE days and nights in Los Muertos, south of La Paz, before crossing the Sea of Cortez to Mazatlan. On our first full day there the weather was very windy and somewhat cold. The next two days, however, were beautiful. We were among three or four other boats in the anchorage. Bordered on the north side by a white sand beach and sand dunes, and flanked by dramatic high hills to the southwest, the bay is very picturesque. The one public facility in Muertos is the Giggling Marlin Beach Club, with good food and fairly reasonable prices, and a view of the bay that can't be beat. Private estates and a golf course are being developed currently, however, leaving us cruisers to wonder if Muertos will soon begin to look and feel like Cabo North.

> **Mazatlan**
>
> *23° 16 N*
> *106° 29 W*
>
> Population: +/- 500,000
>
> Highlight: *If you are looking for a taste of the resort life, spend a couple of nights at Marina El Cid. Guests have access to the two pools, Jacuzzis, restaurant and bar. Laundry services and a shuttle to downtown are available.*

We waited there for three days because our weather report had indicated winds up to 30 knots and seas of 6 feet for our crossing to Mazatlan, so we gave the conditions some time to settle down a bit. We left Friday afternoon at 4:45, and it didn't take long before we were questioning if we had waited too long. The wind was almost nonexistent, which made the rolly seas that much more uncomfortable, reminiscent of that washing machine feeling we've been subjected to before. It didn't improve much over the next 15 hours, although we seemed to make decent headway on our crossing to the other side of the Sea of Cortez.

The rest of the passage continued to be uneventful, and we ended up about seven miles offshore of Mazatlan as the sun was coming up. We were tied up to the fuel dock at Marina El Cid by 8AM, and by 9AM had been assigned to the last available slip in the marina. We quickly caught site of two other boats that were familiar to us- s/v Amalfi, whom we met in La Paz, and s/v So Bella, who we had run into off and on coming down the Baja.

After two days of limited sleep, we were beat. We opted to do nothing more strenuous for the rest of the day than lay by the pool and drink cervezas. El Cid is a mega resort and the pools there are incredible. We spent most of the afternoon occupying real estate beside the pool with Kasey and Amy from s/v Amalfi, and began to feel rejuvenated. Carnival was going on in Mazatlan at the time, so we accepted Kasey and Amy's invitation to accompany them downtown for the evening Carnival parade. The parade was on the malecon, right on the waterfront, and we were lucky enough to get an outside table at a restaurant right at the parade's edge. Mazatlan's Carnival, held annually in late February, is way tamer than those in other parts of the world, and we were nonetheless glad we were there at the right time because it was fun to experience it first hand- lots of music, extravagant floats, dancing, huge crowds – the works.

Monday ended up being boat cleaning, dog washing, and laundry day. By mid afternoon we were pooped and decided to treat ourselves to a dip in the pool and a pina colada. At this point, I was beginning to realize how people end up spending months on end here! We bumped into Darby from s/v So Bella about 5:30 and were invited to join them on their boat for a cocktail. We hadn't seen them since Los Frailles, and ended up swapping stories until 8:30 that evening.

> **TIP:** There are no American-style, do-it-yourself Laundromats in Mexico. You will have to pay to have your laundry done, and it isn't cheap. Keep your expenses down by wearing nylon shorts and other lightweight clothing as much as possible. These things can be washed in the sink with a little Woolite and hung on the lifelines to dry.

On Tuesday we put the dinghy in the water and went for a ride up the channel of the inner harbor. The estates being built back there are quite impressive- kind of like Newport Harbor or Ventura. The word on the docks is that a lot of gringos with money are choosing to retire in Mazatlan. We also checked out Marina Mazatlan during our dinghy ride, which probably would be a fine place to stay if you couldn't get in to El Cid, or had no desire to indulge in the resort lifestyle.

From the log:

Tomorrow we'll take the 40-cent bus into town for groceries and a visit to the bank. We're hoping to leave Mazatlan on Thursday, March 2nd to head south. We're thinking we'll do an overnight passage straight to Isla Isabela, skipping San Blas this trip and stopping there instead on our way back north later this month. We're excited to experience Isla Isabela, a bird refuge and nature preserve that is rumored to have tons of wildlife and amazing snorkeling.

Isla Isabela

WE DIDN'T LEAVE MAZA-TLAN ON March 2nd like I said in the last log entry. Sometimes even the best plans have to be altered. Bryan ended up with Montezuma's revenge, so we stayed at El Cid two more days while he recovered. Once he was feeling better, we made a 20-hour, overnight passage to Isla Isabela, a small island about 50 miles offshore between Mazatlan and Puerto Vallarta.

> **Isla Isabela**
>
> *21° 50.5 N*
> *105° 53 W*
>
> <u>Highlight</u>: *Observing the thousands of frigates and boobies while hiking the foot path, then observing your boat at anchor from high atop the island.*

Isla Isabela is one of Mexico's national parks and is home to numerous wildlife species, most of them in the bird family. It is a bird sanctuary and the annual wintertime birthing destination of frigates and blue, green, and yellow-footed boobies. The place is amazing. Other than the 20 or so fisherman and a handful of researchers living there, it is inhabited only by birds, iguanas, and lizards. You can only get there by boat, and as of now, no tour boats go there. We were one of only six cruising boats in the anchorage, a beautiful place unto itself.

The anchorage is a bit tricky because of the rocky bottom, but with the help of our friend Kasey from s/v Amalfi, who had arrived before us and scouted out the best spots to drop the hook, we ended up setting the anchor in one of the only sandy spots. We had arrived not long after sunrise, and therefore had the whole day to explore. We started off with a dinghy ride around the east side of the island and the "spires," followed by lunch aboard. During our lunch, we heard Amy from Amalfi excitedly calling us over the VHF radio, "Salty Dog, Salty Dog!" It turned out they were trying to reach us to tell us there were pilot whales and a couple of humpback whales putting on a show just outside the anchorage. We jumped in the dinghy, cameras in hand, and rushed out there. We were too late for the pilot whales, but the humpbacks were still doing their thing, raising their tales out of the water and flapping them around, over and over. It was almost like it was the whales' way of waving hello. We floated around in the dinghy for about an hour, admiring God's amazing creatures from a safe distance.

After the whale show, we headed to shore to check out the nature trails and search for the rare blue-footed boobies, who live primarily on the Western coasts of Central and South America, and who make Isla Isabela one of their winter birthing destinations. I was a little uneasy at first because of the number of iguanas and lizards everywhere (I have a small phobia about most things reptilian), but quickly got over it, thankful to have brought along Kasey's trekking poles in case any of them got too close to me! The first birds we noticed were the frigates and their babies, nesting in the trees right at head level. They were EVERYWHERE! But other than frigates and seagulls, we weren't finding any boobies. We chose to take one of the trails that led us through a small valley of calf-high sea grasses, up a tree-dense incline, to a high ledge overlooking the cove 500' below. It was here that we saw our first booby, a colorful yellow-footed one.

We climbed up the path further, and in a thicket of trees we were greeted by a screeching blue-footed booby and her baby. I'm sure she was warning us not to get too close, which of course, we didn't. What an oddly beautiful bird - turquoise blue feet, black and white feathers, and iridescent pale blue eyes. They are about the size and shape of a seagull. With quite a set of lungs, I might add! Up the path even further, we came to a clearing overlooking Crater Lake and with a 360° view of the island. We could see Salty Dog at anchor from there, and the vast Pacific stretching out in all directions beyond. We shot a bunch more photos then headed back to the dinghy, feeling desperately in need of a cold beer and a swim after all that hiking.

Isla Isabela is truly an amazing place. I understand now why Jacques Cousteau and National Geographic have chosen to do features on it. And what's so neat is that Bryan and I have now been to a place where so few people have a chance to go. We got there all by ourselves, on our little 36' sailboat, and this is how we hope it stays... a destination available only to the heartiest travelers among us. Some places just shouldn't be commercialized.

Chacala

From the log: Yeah! We're finally in the tropics!

We arrived at Chacala the following afternoon, March 6th, after a 10-hour crossing from Isla Isabela. It was obvious we had crossed some invisible line into warmer latitudes when the water temperature gauge started reading 82°. Whoopee! Warm water! And then as we approached Chacala from about a mile or so out, there were palm trees and tropical foliage lining the coast in both directions as far as the eye could see. We even saw a few sea turtles, my most favorite of all ocean creatures. This is what I had been dreaming of!

CHACALA IS A VERY PICTURESQUE anchorage. Located about 40 miles north of Puerto Vallarta, the guidebooks describe it as mainly a fishing village, but it also caters to the "snowbird" RV'ers who camp along the beaches during the winter. While definitely not a tourist town (yet), there are 5 or 6 palapa restaurants along the mile-long stretch of beach, as well as a holistic retreat at the southern end of the beach and a couple of hotels in town.

> ### Chacala
>
> *21° 10 N*
> *105° 14.5 W*
>
> <u>Highlight</u>: *With a pretty beach and lots of palm trees, Chacala is often a cruiser's first taste of the tropics. Be sure to enjoy a meal at one of the palapa restaurants on the beach.*

We anchored right off the beach in about 20 feet of water. Us included, there were five cruising boats there. It was a little rolly overnight, but that is a small price to pay for these surroundings. This is the kind of place where it's warm enough to be in a bathing suit from sun up to sundown. You find yourself wanting to play in the water all day, have fish tacos for lunch at one of the palapas on the beach, and finish the day off with a cocktail and some Jimmy Buffett music while lounging in the cockpit. It's fabulous.

The next day, after a leisurely morning of walking the dogs along the beach and having breakfast aboard, we made our way to "town." We walked down a couple of Chacala's stone streets in a residential neighborhood, past a small church with beautiful stained glass windows, and ended up on the "main" street just one block off the beach. The main drag is lined on both sides with local souvenir vendors and more restaurants than you would expect in a town this size. We stopped in at "Koko Bongo's," lured there by a $3 cheeseburger/fries/drink special, internet, and CNN on the TV. Who would have thought! The proprietor of this business obviously knows what gringos are suckers for! The town reminded me a little of Jaco or Quepos in Costa Rica back in the mid-nineties, before those places became so popular with Americans. I should revise that - it reminds me of those places, but without the bugs! We weren't bothered by mosquitoes or no-see-ums here, but it might just have been the time of year.

> **TIP: Burn a citronella candle or mosquito coil in your cockpit to keep the bugs away. (The mosquito coil can be placed in the bottom of an old coffee can to keep it from burning too fast). Inside the boat, burning incense also helps.**

After lunch, we ventured out to one of the palapas on the beach for a beer and to watch the world go by. We were joined by Dick and Judy from s/v Boundless, our neighbors in the anchorage. We had a really nice chat with them for awhile before heading back to the boat to get the dogs for their evening walk. Incidentally, their walk turned out to be quite an adventure. We hadn't picked the best spot to beach the dinghy, and ended up making a less than graceful exit from the beach through the breaking surf. What's wrong with this picture?! This has happened to us too many times before. You'd think we would have learned a thing or two by that point! Oh well, at least we gave all those people on the beach something to laugh about.

La Cruz, Banderas Bay

THE MOTOR SAIL FROM CHACALA to Punta de Mita, the landmark for the northern end of Banderas Bay, was very warm and pleasant. Definitely bathing suit weather. We followed the advice of the cruising guides and swung wide around the point to avoid the rocky patch that sits within a mile of the shore. It was easy to spot because of the surf breaking over the rocks. As soon as we changed course to begin heading east, we got a little taste of the breeze that makes Banderas Bay so famous for its sailing. In fact, in the distance we could see quite a few racing sailboats, with their spinnakers flying, heading back into the marinas of Puerto Vallarta and Nuevo Vallarta. We wouldn't be following them in, however. We were headed to the anchorage at La Cruz, almost ten miles to the west of the big (and expensive) town of Puerto Vallarta.

La Cruz

20° 45 N
105° 23 W

<u>Highlight</u>: *As of 2008, a new marina with all modern amenities was being constructed.*

www.marinarivieranayarit.com

After reading about our time in Chacala, you know how much we enjoyed our time there. You may be expecting our thoughts about La Cruz, a mere 30 miles by land from Chacala, would be more of the same - a tropical setting, lots of palm trees, and palapas on the beach. Alas, what a difference 30 miles can make!

La Cruz is night-and-day different from Chacala. Like Chacala, La Cruz is also a fishing village, but it doesn't have the quaint feel of a rustic little beach town. La Cruz isn't very tropical at all, mostly dusty and dry, and more reminiscent of a Baja fishing village than it is like Chacala. At the time that we were there, there was a small breakwater that sheltered an inner harbor. The inner harbor was the home of quite a few fishing pangas and a few assorted working class vessels belonging to the locals. All the cruising sailboats were anchored outside of the breakwater in about 20' of water.

The beach in La Cruz is not all that inviting. Outside the breakwater, the beach is fairly steep, the water is not all that clean, and the sand is littered with trash. We had to venture to this crummy beach twice a day to walk our dogs, but were constantly on watch to make sure Sadie and Fletch weren't eating any of the trash or dead fish parts that were lying around. Inside the breakwater, there was a stretch of beach where cruisers who wanted to walk to town could beach their dingies. Beaching the dinghy was fairly easy in the morning, when the water was calm, but much more difficult in the afternoon when La Cruz's infamous winds would start blowing, turning up the chop and a little bit of surf at the dinghy landing. Generally, the trip from the landing back out to the boat involved everyone getting fairly wet. The wind would also stir up the sand of the town, blowing it out into the anchorage and coating the sailboats in a layer of dirt. The one *good* thing about the wind is that it kept the insects away.

So unlike Chacala, there definitely weren't any cute little palapa restaurants on the beach here. Don't get me wrong, though. La Cruz has its benefits. It is a cruiser's hangout, for sure. A pleasant alternative to the costly marinas of Puerto Vallarta a couple hours sail from here, there are at least 40 sailboats in the anchorage at any given time during the cruising season. Half of these boats are on their way to the South Pacific, the other half are heading north into the Sea of Cortez, which makes for some interesting people to talk to. We were happy to have run into many cruising friends here - s/v Moorea and s/v Simplicity, for example - and thoroughly enjoyed our chance to spend time with them once again.

Another benefit of La Cruz is the cruiser-friendly businesses started by ex-cruisers here who have chosen to make La Cruz their home. Our favorite of these is "Fox's Beans and Buns." Fox, the proprietor, truly embodies the entrepreneurial spirit. One morning last fall as he sat on his shaded patio, some cruisers walked by and asked where they could get a good cup of coffee in town. "Nowhere," he had to tell them. The same thing happened a couple more times, so he started inviting the cruisers to join him on his patio for a cup of his favorite organic Mexican coffee. Soon the word spread, so he started selling muffins and cinnamon rolls to the ever-increasing crowd. Next came full breakfasts prepared by his partner, Silvia, and wireless internet service (the only one in La Cruz). Then free phone service to call the U.S. or Canada. Now Fox and Silvia are doing a booming business *every morning*, and they do it on their front patio in shorts, t-shirts, and bare feet. Isn't that the coolest story you've heard in awhile?! But to their credit, they saw a need and they filled it. And cruiser's who come to La Cruz are extremely grateful.

But La Cruz as most people have known it is changing. As we write this, a marina is under construction. Many local homeowners and fishermen fear that they are going to be forced to relocate. The consensus among those we have talked to is that the whole feel of the town will change, and people are divided on how they feel about it. This includes cruisers, because rumor has it that the anchorage here may no longer be free. If that is the case, there would no longer be any safe and comfortable overnight anchorages in Banderas Bay, with the exception of Punta de Mita on the extreme northwest corner of the bay. What will come from the growth in La Cruz remains to be seen, but we hope everyone's interests can be met.

Chapter 7

Sea Of Cortez

Making Memories

Back In La Paz

W E STAYED IN LA CRUZ for one week, making trips into Puerto Vallarta for provisions and exploration, and spending time with friends from S/v Moorea and S/v Simplicity. Bryan and I were feeling anxious to begin heading back north, and then back across the Sea, as we were expecting Bryan's parents and a couple of friends from home to rendezvous with us in La Paz during the first week of April. We would have liked to spend more time in this region and check out the rest of the popular spots, and were sorry we hadn't headed to Mexico's Pacific coast sooner in the year.

So we set off north, stopping again in Chacala to spend a couple more nights there. Everyone we talked to told us how uncomfortable their time in San Blas had been because of the mosquitoes, so we opted to skip that stop between Chacala and Mazatlan. After a couple of days in Mazatlan reprovisioning the boat, we started back across the Sea of Cortez. The weather was fine, but the trip proved to be a special one. Like us, many other boats were taking advantage of the good weather to make the crossing, and we heard quite a few of them chatting on the VHF our first night out. One of the captains set up an informal cruiser's net on one of the channels, and we were all able to check in with one another regularly over the next 24 hours and share important information about other boats coming our direction, like the large ferry that crosses from La Paz to Mazatlan. It was on this trip that we first heard of the boats s/v Godspeed and s/v Jakyra, the cruisers on which would later turn out to be some of our favorite cruising buddies.

Bryan and I were very excited to have visitors during our first week back in La Paz. Dave & Barb, Bryan's parents, and our good friends Jason and Carrie left the cold and rainy weather of Southern California to spend a week relaxing in the warmth of Mexico. And boy, did they relax! In fact, on a couple of occasions, Barb was overheard saying how much she *didn't* want to go home.

Of course, we did a lot of the expected laying around in the sun, eating great food, and souvenir shopping, but the highlight of their stay with us was our two days on the water. On the second day of their trip, we chartered the 47' catamaran "Windsong" from our friend Captain Ron for a day at the islands. On our way out of the marina, we were greeted by a large pod of dolphin, who hung around the boat for about 20 minutes, playing in the bow wake. Awesome. Our first stop was at Los Islotes, a small collection of rocky pinnacles north of Isla Partida, where we were able to swim with the resident sea lions. It was a little unnerving at first to have rather large sea lions whizzing by you, seeming somewhat aggressive. Once we got used to it, it was great fun – one of those once in a lifetime kind of experiences. It was as though the sea lions were putting on an underwater ballet dance just for our enjoyment.

Our final stop that afternoon was at Bahia San Gabriel on Isla Espirtu Santo, a large crescent-shaped bay with crystal clear, teal green water and uninhabited beaches. Again, there wasn't another soul around and we had the whole bay to ourselves. The guys couldn't resist the opportunity to jump in the water and paddle around for awhile before lunch. To satisfy the huge appetites we all had worked up, Captain Ron prepared yummy cheeseburgers on the BBQ, and we all sat around relishing the chance to have our cheeseburgers in paradise. Later we took the dinghy to shore and had a stroll along the beautiful white sand beach before the captain signaled that it was time to weigh anchor and return to the marina. It was an amazing day of family and fun on the water.

A couple days later we were blessed again with fabulous weather and decided to spend that day on the water, as well. We loaded up Salty Dog with provisions and spent the day anchored at Balandra Cove, one of our favorite spots in the La Paz area. Even though there were a few other boats in the cove, we felt like we had the place all to ourselves and explored the beach for a couple of hours without ever running into another person. After all that exercise, we ventured back to the boat for a lunch of barbequed chicken and salad, which was followed up by a whole lot of laying around, and you guessed it, more relaxing! It was great to see our friends and family fully appreciating "manana time."

The end of their visit arrived too quickly and our guests had to return to California. However, Bryan and I are so thankful that they were able to have a little taste of our cruising life in Mexico. We only hope that they all enjoyed their time with us as much as we enjoyed having them visit.

La Paz to Loreto

AFTER A FAIRLY LAZY WEEK of laying around the pool at the marina and adjusting to the ever-increasing temperatures, we were ready to head north, further up into the Sea of Cortez. So on April 16th we finally started prepping the boat for departure and saying good-bye to friends. We had Rob and Kat over to Salty Dog for Easter brunch in the morning, and later that evening we barbequed aboard Windsong with Ron, Fred, Redmond, Tracy & Julie, Kasey and Rob & Kat. The

> **Puerto Escondido**
> *(approx 12 miles SSE of Loreto)*
>
> 25° 48.5 N
> 111° 18 W
>
> <u>Highlight</u>: *This very large, nearly land-locked all-weather anchorage can accommodate over 100 boats. (This could change if the proposed marina is ever built.)*
>
> *Minimal provisions and ice can be purchased approximately 1 mile up the main road.*

following day, after spending a significant amount of time grocery shopping and storing food and drinks on board, we were invited to Kasey's boat for arrachera and all the fixings. Other than Kasey, who would hopefully catch up with us by the time we reached Puerto Escondido, we wouldn't see many of these friends again for another couple of months.

While saying good-bye to old friends is always a bummer, hanging out with new cruising friends is largely what made the time in Mexico so enjoyable for Bryan and me. In March, on our crossing from Mazatlan to Los Muertos, we ended up making the 36 hour passage with two other boats, s/v Godspeed and s/v Jakyrah, whom we hadn't previously met. We all rendezvoused in Los Muertos and after hearing us describe how great Marina Costa Baja is, they too decided to check in there for a few weeks. Over those weeks we got to know each other better and discovered how much we have in common. Leonard and Beth from Godspeed not only had their boat near ours in San Pedro prior to heading to Mexico, but their permanent residence is in Phelan, an area of the High Desert near where Bryan and I are from. They even know some of the same High Desert people we do! San Diegans Tom and Chris from Jakyrah just retired from their jobs in education, where he was a middle school counselor and she was a PE teacher. Wow, what a small world!

On April 18th, Godspeed, Jakyrah and Salty Dog left La Paz to buddy boat north to Loreto. Our first stop was Partida Cove on Isla Partida, 20 miles from La Paz. After getting the boats anchored that afternoon, we all enjoyed rum and cokes together aboard Jakyrah. The following day Bryan, Tom, and Leonard felt the urge to do something manly, and decided a good way to get in some male bonding would be to go diving for scallops. Despite the cold water and the challenge of breaking the scallops free from the rocks, the guys came back with a large catch. We were able to BBQ that night on Beth and Leonard's boat, gorging ourselves on delectable bacon-wrapped scallops.

The next day we sailed the six hours to San Evaristo, our anchorage for the next two nights. Again, we spent our evenings having dinner together and socializing. Bryan and Tom developed a knack for teasing one another, much to the amusement of the rest of us. It's this kind of companionship and socializing that makes cruising so fun. Tom & Chris and Beth & Leonard, like most cruisers, are some of the friendliest, most helpful people you'll ever meet, and Bryan and I are so thankful to have met them. Beth and Leonard even gained nicknames, and from that point on were affectionately referred to as "Ma and Pa Godspeed."

Caleta Partida and San Evaristo are nice anchorages, but Los Gatos and Agua Verde, further north, are even nicer. Los Gatos is a medium-sized cove ringed by a pretty beach and spectacular pink and peach sandstone cliffs. In the distance to the west of the anchorage, dramatic tall mountains and peaks rise up and give you the feeling you're in the Grand Canyon. Agua Verde, our last stop before we reached Puerto Escondido, is slightly less remote than Los Gatos but in my opinion is equally as nice. The cove lacks the bright pink sandstone cliffs, but the green of the palm trees and other native plants growing along the beach makes up for that, as does the emerald green water of the anchorage.

> **TIP: Support the local economy in Aqua Verde by purchasing homemade tortillas from the tortillaria in town. In Los Gatos, the panga fishermen appreciate donations of school supplies for their children.**

After five fabulous days in Agua Verde, where we passed the time fishing, exploring, and cocktailing, all three boats left together on the morning of April 29th, bound for Puerto Escondido. We arrived in the middle of the afternoon and found a nice spot to anchor about halfway up the cove from the narrow entrance to the south. We were all a bit surprised at how huge Puerto Escondido is, with a capacity for a couple hundred boats. The Spanish translation for Puerto Escondido is "hidden port," a very appropriate name for this cove. It's very well protected and rarely does any swell find its way into the anchorage. The only drawbacks are the absence of a decent beach to walk the dogs and a lack of services nearby. A roundtrip taxi into Loreto, a mere 13 miles away, costs a whopping $65!!! Ouch! But we found ourselves making this trip twice, as we needed to do things in town such as visit the bank, the grocery store, and immigration. Not much we could do about the cost, but we thankfully had friends to split it with.

From the log:

In total, we spent ten days in Puerto Escondido. "Loreto Fest" was going on while we were there and the harbor was full of boats from all over the Sea of Cortez. We ran into many cruisers we had previously met along the way and enjoyed the chance to get caught up with them. Now we're on to destinations further north - Isla Carmen, San Juanico, and probably Conception Bay. It's hard to believe our time in Mexico is winding down, but by June 1st we'll be back in La Paz to put the boat away for the summer. I guess time really does fly when you're having rum! I mean fun!

Ballandra Cove at Isla Carmen

WE LEFT PUERTO ESCONDIDO AND motored to Isla Carmen with our friends on s/v Amalfi and s/v Godspeed. It was an easy trip, a mere 14 miles, which took us a little over 3 hours. We anchored in Ballandra Cove with about 12 other boats. Ballandra is a nice cove with lots of beach for the dogs to run on and a nightly view of the city lights of Loreto, seven miles to the west.

> *From the log: We've been sort of lazy yesterday and today... it's so hot that you don't want to do much. We've played with the dogs on the beach (little Sadie has suddenly decided that she likes to swim and she's so much fun to watch as she splashes in the water and chases fish), taken a couple of dinghy rides, and played dominoes in our shaded cockpit.*

Our first full day in Ballandra Cove was a very special one. Bryan and I had one of those awesome experiences that makes spending time in the Sea of Cortez so memorable. We borrowed kayaks from Beth and Leonard and paddled out beyond the point on the northwest end of the anchorage. We were in an area of rocks and reefs and were literally surrounded by wildlife. We saw two seagulls on the beach with their three young chicks, whose black and gray feathers perfectly camouflaged them to match the surrounding rocks. We spotted bright red crabs, blue, gray and red starfish, stingrays the size of boogie boards, and a swimming eel. The highlight of the morning, however, was the variety and number of fish. At one point, as I hovered in my kayak over a rocky area with crystal clear water all around, I was surrounded by hundreds and hundreds of tropical fish. I spotted angel fish, needle fish, trigger fish, sergeant majors, and about ten other brightly colored varieties that I don't know the names of. For about 15 minutes I sat mesmerized by the shades of blue, orange, and yellow swirling all around me. Some of the fish were feeding on the surface about six inches from my hand. There was no wind, not even the hint of a breeze, and the water was perfectly still.

It was quiet- so quiet in fact that the silence was interrupted only by the swooshing of the pelican's wings, occasionally passing overhead. Nature's harmony... what a beautiful thing.

> **TIP:** Spring and Summer temperatures in the Sea of Cortez are very warm. Make a point of installing 12 volt fans in your galley, sleeping quarters, and heads. You'll be glad you did!

San Juanico and the "Aquatic Landmine"

*H*AH!! THE HARMONY OF NATURE - I can't help but laugh at the irony of it.

Just two days after writing that piece about the idyllic conditions at Isla Carmen, we arrived, along with our friends on s/v Amalfi and s/v Godspeed, at San Juanico Cove, on the Baja about 25 miles north of Loreto. Like the last place we visited, this cove is very picturesque, and the white sand beach beckoned us. We put the dinghy in the water, loaded up the dogs, and headed to shore. The water was refreshing, about 78°, and all of us were cooling off, even little Sadie, who within the last couple of days had decided she's a swimmer. We were having such a nice time, playing in the water with the dogs, when we were joined on the beach by Beth and Leonard, who had dingied over to join in on the fun.

Standing in knee-deep water, I turned to walk to the beach to greet Beth and Leonard and WHAM! Something started thrashing about under my feet. I suddenly felt intense pain, mixed with a strong dose of fear. The water was so churned up I couldn't see what was in the water below me. My foot hurt so bad... I started screaming to Bryan... *Oh my God*, I was thinking, *I have to get out of the water, but I can't walk!* I couldn't put pressure on my left foot. Bryan scooped me up under my arms and got me to the dinghy. The inner arch of my left foot had a one inch vertical gash in it and it was bleeding like crazy. It had been less than sixty seconds since the event, but there was already so much blood. Bryan rinsed off my foot and applied pressure to stop the bleeding, and I kept thinking how thankful I was at that moment that he was formerly an EMT. Holy crap, what happened?! Was that a stingray in the water? I guess it must have been, but I never saw a thing.

Oh man, my foot was *really* hurting. And bleeding. Bryan tried desperately to get me to calm down. I was on the verge of tears, although I'm not sure if that was mostly due to the pain, the sight of all that blood, or the realization of how far we were from a hospital at that moment. Probably all of the above. Needing to get back out to the boat for first aid supplies, Leonard helped Bryan load me and the dogs back into the dinghy. No small task with me freaking out about the dogs, worried about one of them encountering a stingray, too.

Back at the boat, but not really knowing what to do for my injury, we found the paragraph about stingrays in our first aid book. Hot water! It said to immerse the injury immediately in hot water, as hot as the person can tolerate. We put my foot in a bucket and did as instructed. The bleeding was subsiding, but the pain was increasing. How is this possible!!? It already hurt so much! As the extremely hot water was drawing the venom out of the wound and I could see it trickling in a bloody ooze from my foot, I started to cry. I have never felt such pain. And it was getting worse, not better.

Word about what had happened to me started to spread around the anchorage. Kasey came over and brought some antibiotic ointments he found in his medicine cabinet. Our friend Tracy from s/v *Eagle Dancer* delivered an Epsom salt-like mixture to put in my bucket of hot water. It turns out that during the previous season they were anchored near a lady who got stung by a stingray and who used the same stuff. Gino and Pat from s/v *Chalet Mer*, whom we had never previously met, stopped by. Pat was stung six months earlier in Muertos and they knew what needed to be done. They came aboard, looked at my wound, gave Bryan instructions about digging out the barb (which was still in my foot), and hurried back to their boat to get me some medicine. Pat and Gino informed us that antibiotics need to be started right away, otherwise a staph or strep infection can set in. Gino and Pat returned right away with the medicine, demonstrating the compassion and generosity that is so common among cruisers. They supervised while Bryan removed five pieces of the stingray's barb from my still-oozing wound. Pat encouraged me to take something for the pain, and I was thankful that we had Vicodin on board.

A couple hours passed and I was still soaking my foot. The pain was still excruciating. Every time Bryan added new hot water to the bucket, thus causing more venom to come trickling out of the wound, the discomfort kicked up a bit more. I vividly remember commenting to him that I didn't have nearly so much pain after the surgery I had the previous year.

Beth and Leonard came over to check on me. While they are there, I was overcome by nausea and dizziness, probably from the Vicodin I took. Beth put a cool washcloth on my forehead and the symptoms started to go away.

After a few hours of soaking my foot and a bit of good 'ole Vicodin in my system, I started to feel better. Thank goodness. I don't know how anyone could get through more than a few hours of such pain without passing out. Bryan moved me inside, got me situated on the couch with my foot elevated, and made me some dinner. Afterwards, I quickly fell asleep.

By the next morning, I was doing much better. My foot didn't hurt much at all, but it was really swollen. I had to take it easy most of the day. I began to realize that it wasn't all that surprising this happened, considering how much time we had spent in the water over the last eight months. I'm very thankful it didn't happen to one of the dogs, and from then on we were much more alert when we took them to shore.

From the log:

It has been 15 days since I stepped on that dumb stingray, and my foot is finally doing better. It was swollen and painful to walk on for the first five days. I was lulled into a false sense of security after the sixth day when it started feeling much better, and went walking around the ghost town at Bahia Salinas with Bryan and some friends, and additionally got my feet wet at the beach. I guess I did too much too soon, because the next day I had a relapse which lasted for five more days. The swelling was bad, and I had to elevate my foot at least a couple times a day.

I hobbled around the boat because it hurt to walk. I had been advised that the wound would take a long time to heal, but I didn't know how long that really meant. Now I do. Two weeks for the swelling to subside and a minimum of three to four weeks for the wound to close up. It's a good thing I don't have to wear shoes anytime soon!

After reading up on the subject, we now know that stingray injuries are quite common in the Sea of Cortez, although they can happen anywhere. We've also read that the power of their sting is likened to that of an "aquatic landmine," which I agree is a pretty accurate description. Wearing shoes in the water and doing the "stingray shuffle" while you walk are helpful but not foolproof against stingrays.

TIP: If you are stung by a stingray, rinse the wound with clean, fresh water (not sea water) as soon as possible and soak it in water as hot as 113° for at least 90 minutes to draw out the venom. Remove any pieces of the barb or other debris with sterile tweezers. Start a five day regimen of antibiotics to ward off infection. Apply a sterile dressing to the wound each day for the first few days. Stay out of the saltwater for at least a week, longer is advisable. Saltwater has traces of bacteria in it that can cause infection.

Heading Home...

AFTER MY ENCOUNTER WITH THE unfriendly stingray in San Juanico and a few days of taking it easy to facilitate recovery, we headed south to Isla Carmen on May 15th. Along with s/v Godspeed and s/v Eagle Dancer, we anchored at La Lancha Cove at the north end of the island. The next morning we explored the northeast part of the island by dinghy and found some of Isla Carmen's famed caves. The most impressive was at tiny but beautiful V-Neck Cove and was large enough for at least three dinghies. We were joined in the anchorage later that day by s/v Amalfi, and we all ended up having dinner together that night on Godspeed. Kasey had been absent from the group for a few days, so it felt good to have our flotilla of friends back together.

May 17th found us at Bahia Salinas on the east side of Isla Carmen. Traveling with Godspeed and Amalfi, we chose to spend one night here so we could explore the 200 year old ruins at the Salinas ghost town, a former sea salt operation. The ghost town isn't very large- we walked the whole thing in under an hour- but it was interesting to see the old offices (which still had files in the filing cabinet!), the church, school, Pharmacia, and so forth.

By May 18th, we started our journey south and "home" to La Paz. We took ten leisurely days to do so, with stops in Puerto Escondido, Agua Verde, Los Gatos, Evaristo, and Isla Partida, arriving back in La Paz on May 28th. It was good to be back and see the friends we had missed. While we wished we did not need to leave, we had discovered during our travels through Mexico that it would not be legal for us to try to work there. Even with a captain's license, Bryan could not work as a boat captain in Mexico due to their law that only Mexican citizens can be employed as skippers. Because we had spent most of our savings, we decided to return home and work for awhile, which left us to begin the process of getting the boat ready to leave it at Marina Costa Baja for the summer and hurricane season. That involved many tasks, not the least of which was removing all the sails and canvas, as well as cleaning everything inside and out. The hot, hot temperatures made getting work done extremely uncomfortable, and we were thankful we could go to the marina pool in the afternoons to cool off.

In the process of all the prep work, Bryan and I found ourselves reflecting on the highlights of our trip. It's interesting that while we came up with our sentiments separately, they are surprisingly similar. Hands down, the most memorable aspect of our eight months in Mexico were the incredible people we met and the lifelong friendships that were made. Additionally, we relished our days unencumbered by alarm clocks and schedules, being free to play when we wanted to, rest when we needed it, and spend quality time with each other, our dogs, and our friends. Exploring Mexico and building our skills as sailors was great, but the benefits of those things were outweighed by the health, happiness, and rejuvenation that our cruising life gave us. The greatest challenge at this point was trying to prepare ourselves emotionally for our return to the States and the "rat race" that we feared may once again surround us. Additionally, we were warned by veteran cruisers to expect a bit of culture shock when we got home.

While it was strange to think about leaving all this, even just temporarily, we *were* anxious to head home. We missed our families and friends in California very much and couldn't wait to be with them again. For us, people and relationships are what life is all about, and it made us happy to know we'd be around for the births, family events, birthdays, and good times that were to happen that summer. Yet at the same time, we were conflicted. We would think about friends and loved ones who dream of doing what we had been lucky enough to do, and we wanted to say to them "GO FOR IT!" Don't wait, because the chance may pass you by.

Our trip home involved some inconvenience, both financial and physical. We couldn't fly home because of the dogs, and for the same reason we couldn't take the bus. We eventually decided to rent a car in La Paz and drive it to Ensenada at a cost of $700. We thought the drive would be an "adventure," but discovered that the interior of the

Baja isn't all that exciting and the roads are just slightly better than okay. Because driving at night isn't recommended, we had to plan our trip around two overnight stops, Loreto and Guerrero Negro. In Loreto we were able to find a nice pet-friendly hotel, but we weren't so lucky in Guerrero Negro. We ended up in a flee-bag motel room, the kind where you feel more comfortable sleeping *on top* of the covers.

Once back in California, we most definitely experienced the culture shock that those more experienced cruisers in La Paz had warned us about. We were soon wishing we could go back to the more peaceful kind of life we had enjoyed aboard Salty Dog, but had to stay put and try to make some money. We found ourselves feeling very envious of those cruisers who are fortunate to have large enough retirement incomes that they can cruise as often and as long as they want without having to return to work.

We had hoped to be able to go back to Mexico in November to sail Salty Dog home, but weren't able to because of work commitments. It became obvious to us that we were done with our cruising adventures, at least for the time being. This left us with a dilemma, though. We had to get Salty Dog back home to California.

Chapter 8

Bashing Up The Baja

April 2007

Return to La Paz!!

Yes, it's true. After ten months of being back home in California, we came to realize that we would not financially be able to return to Mexico for another cruising season. Bryan and I therefore knew we needed to return to La Paz and bring Salty Dog back to her home waters. We had missed her so much. Living aboard and cruising for a year most definitely made her feel like part of the family. I suppose that sounds a bit silly to non-boaters... I don't know if RV'ers get emotionally attached to their motor homes, for instance. But on a sailboat, making 2-3 day passages offshore, completely out of sight of land, and totally at the mercy of Mother Nature, you end up putting a great deal of trust in your vessel to safely deliver you to your destination. Salty Dog had been good to us, and like I said, we missed her.

We also didn't want Salty Dog to go through another hurricane season in Mexico. She rode out Hurricane John during the summer of 2006 while in her slip in La Paz, and while she came through it unscathed, Bryan and I were nervous wrecks back home in California, glued to the weather updates on the internet like a couple of neurotic parents. Friends would say to us, "It doesn't really matter if the boat sinks, though, does it? It's insured, right? You could just get a new one." They just don't get it, I guess.

We arrived in La Paz on April 2nd to put the boat back together and start our journey home. It was bittersweet to be back in Marina Costa Baja, home to so many great memories for us. Our good friends Beth and Leonard from Godspeed were there, as was Kasey from Amalfi, one of our favorite cruising friends. We all shared a few meals and the requisite rum and cokes together, enjoying each others company once again. We were feeling sad about leaving them, and we'd only been back in Pa Paz for a couple of days.

We got a big surprise on Thursday morning as Beth and I were heading into town to do some provisioning. She and Leonard somewhat skeptically announced that they had decided to sail Godspeed home to California, as well. We would be going north together. What?!?! We had no idea they were even considering making the trip. But plans change, and they were ready to return to California, and this way we could buddy boat and keep an eye on each other. This was really exciting news. We were honestly a bit stunned though, because like me, Beth had always been quite vocal about not wanting to do the Baja Bash. (The "Bash" is the nickname given by cruisers to the trip up the Baja, and is a reference to the conditions frequently experienced.) She admitted, though, that if she had to do it, she'd only make the trip if they had another boat to partner up with. And quite honestly, I was extremely relieved to be going with another boat, as well. The "bash" (which we renamed "the bliss" in hopes of bringing good karma our way) is known for being one heck of an unpleasant trip. I was glad to know we would not be out there alone if we got into any trouble.

Two days later both boats were ready to go and we set out for the first leg of the trip from La Paz to Cabo San Lucas. After a rough first few hours, the winds and seas calmed down, and we began our first overnight passage in almost a year. Having not done an overnighter in a while, Bryan and I were a bit rusty, and found it a little difficult to find our on-watch, off-watch rhythm. But Sunday morning dawned bright and sunny, and on my morning watch a few hours out of Cabo, I was feeling nostalgic, and found myself writing in the log about the first time we approached the tip of the Baja Peninsula, almost a year and a half earlier.

> *Getting back into the swing of night passages last night was a little tough. I had forgotten how exhausting it can be! Thank goodness the conditions were mild. When I got up this morning around 8AM, Bryan went back to sleep. He's pooped. We're about 2 hours north of Cabo and I can see the arches from here.*

I remember what a joyous day it was for us when we rounded those arches for the first time in December 2005 with the S/v Blackwood as our buddy boat. After 3 weeks coming down the Baja, the civilization of Cabo was a welcome sight. It feels different this time, going the other direction. We're all anxious, because we just want to get home as quickly as possible and as comfortably as possible. And we're a tad apprehensive, because we're not as naive as we were the first time. We know what kind of conditions we might get out there, although we're praying that it's just calm and blissful.

It's also different this time because we don't have the dogs with us. I miss them. But I'm glad they won't have to make the trip north. It will be a lot easier on all of us this way. It's just odd not to have them underfoot all the time.

We pulled into the gas dock in Cabo around 12:30 PM. Both boats fueled up, and despite some wind and choppy seas, decided to continue on and get around the infamous Cabo Falso on our push to Mag Bay.

BAM!! As soon as we got around the arches, it was time for foul weather gear. It was rough, wet, and really, really slow. Poor Captain Bryan was absolutely drenched from the spray coming over the bow. Oh well, we were in it by then and there was no use turning around. We beat into the swells and wind for a few hours, and then thankfully it started to flatten out just a bit. The current was really cranking and we felt like we were going nowhere fast. We took a more offshore route and s/v Godspeed stayed close to shore. Although we didn't intend it, we lost radio contact with one another before nightfall because the distance between us got to be too great. Not a good feeling. Your brain starts to do funny things. But we pushed those worried thoughts aside and pressed on, and 48 hours after leaving Cabo we arrived in Bahia Santa Maria. Much to our disbelief, we were the only boat there. No s/v Godspeed. And no radio contact from them for the last 40 hours. We figured they would have been four or five hours ahead of us. Oh no, here come those bad thoughts again. Bryan and I started second guessing ourselves, wondering if maybe we misunderstood and were supposed to pull into Mag Bay instead? But we stuck with what we thought was the plan and dropped the anchor to wait for our buddy boat to arrive.

Bahia Santa Maria, one of our most favorite anchorages in November 2005, was completely blown out on that particular day in 2007. Huge, rolling swell inside the anchorage, and massive breakers on the beach. What we had remembered as a picturesque and quiet anchorage in 2005 was now the place of crashing waves that sounded like thunder. No chance of us going to shore in the dinghy, that's for sure!

We ate some lunch and took showers, which felt pretty amazing after 48 hours in the same yucky clothes and salt-crusted foul weather gear. We laid down and tried to nap, which lasted only about ten minutes. The swells were so large under our boat that we'd ride up on one wave, pulling the anchor chain under the boat, and then ride down the backside of the wave, pulling the chain tight again, causing a deafening chafing-like noise on the bow roller. Yikes! We were up like a flash and outside in an instant. The swells were building even more now. There were double breakers on the beach. And still no Godspeed. Bryan started to get that look on his face, the one that tells me he's having an uneasy feeling in his gut. Not good. Just as I was observing his troubled look, he spoke up and said "We should go. If the swells continue to build", he explained, "we could be in trouble." And, he said, maybe if we went into Mag Bay we'd find s/v Godspeed there. Now, I know I'm not the world's most experienced cruiser, but I've spent enough time on the water to know that if the skipper gets a feeling about something, you go with it. You don't wait around, hemming and hawing. We have gut feelings for a reason.

We picked up the anchor, exhausted as we were, and headed into Mag Bay around 2:45 PM. We knew it would be at least four hours before we dropped the hook again. And we would kind of be going backwards, the wrong way down the Baja, but at least we could get some protection from the seas.

Around 5PM, like music to our ears, s/v Godspeed hailed us on the radio. They were outside of Mag Bay, about four or five miles from us, and could see us on the horizon when we were high on the top of a swell. Thank God! We had been somewhat seriously considering if we would need to contact the Coast Guard or Mexican Navy, so hearing their voices was honestly like a thousand pound weight had been lifted from us. It turns out they had gotten a bit beaten up following the coastal track and hadn't made good time. Just as we had been worried about them, they had been worried sick about us. They changed course and followed us in to Mag Bay. Together, both boats were gratefully at anchor around 8PM in Man 'O War Cove, about eight miles north from the entrance to Mag Bay. Here it was beautifully flat and calm, allowing us all to get a much needed full night's rest.

Man 'O War Cove,
Magdalena Bay to Abreojos
The frustration begins...

WEDNESDAY MORNING, MAN 'O WAR Cove, inside Mag Bay... There were five other boats here in addition to us and s/v Godspeed - three sailboats, one catamaran, and 1 trawler. We met with the port captain, "Gregory," for check in. This formality isn't required anywhere else in Mexico, but it's required in Man 'O War, so you just go with the flow. We ordered 40 gallons of diesel from him to be delivered the next day, and then dingied over to visit with Beth and Leonard. For most of the day we rested up, and then had a chicken dinner aboard s/v Godspeed. It was at dinner that night that Beth entertained us with her telling of how cold and miserable she was on the trip from Cabo, and that she had a new way to stay warm and keep from getting sick. She would lay on the floor in their salon because the heat radiating up through the floorboards from the engine below would warm her, and it was the spot where the least amount of motion was felt.

On Thursday we dingied over to introduce ourselves to s/v Flame, whose owners are Paul and Debbie, from Ventura. Later that afternoon they invited everyone "vacationing" in Man 'O War cove to their boat for cocktails. We attended, of course, as did Beth and Leonard, and Joe and Kathy from s/v Katy Kat. Everyone brought snacks. We got to know each other, checked out Paul and Debbie's J40, and talked about our weather concerns. Before we departed for the evening, we all agreed to talk again the next day to compare weather notes.

After each boat listened to the Amigo net Friday morning and heard Don's doom and gloom forecast for the next week, Joe invited everyone to his catamaran, s/v Katy Kat, for coffee and a strategy session. We picked up Beth and Leonard, but it was really windy and choppy in the anchorage, and after we all got soaked traveling the short distance between Salty Dog and Godspeed, Beth and I opted to forego the rest of the trip to s/v Katy Kat and stayed aboard. The guys beat their way the remaining 100 yards to Joe and Kathy's boat while we visited on Salty Dog and tried to warm up. While we were waiting for them to return, my mom called on the cell phone (technology is great!) to give us the weather info she could pull off the BajaInsider. com website. Her info was much more encouraging than Don's. The guys returned from the weather pow-wow and confirmed that they, too, were getting much more positive readings from the weather fax and grib files that Paul and Joe were able to download. Consensus was that we would leave in the pre-dawn hours on Saturday for Turtle Bay.

We all left Man'O War around 4:30 AM the next day – s/v Godspeed, s/v Flame, Paul on s/v Casablanca, s/v Solitude, s/v Katy Kat, and us. The first twelve or so hours were fine, and we even were able to motorsail at about 5.5 - 6.0 knots. Nightfall brought a little more chop, but still an okay ride. By early morning, the conditions had taken a drastic turn for the worse.

From the log, April 15, 2007

Well, it has been another night out in the crap. Cold. Wind on the nose. Uncomfortable seas. Seems like a pattern! Nightfall didn't bring any relief. Everybody in our caravan is tired. Not sure yet if we'll be pressing on to Turtle Bay, or pulling in somewhere for relief.

I went on watch just before 6 AM, and by 7 AM, as the sun was coming up, the wind and seas really began to pick up. At 7 AM, I felt it necessary to wake up Bryan to assess the conditions. It wasn't but ten minutes later that we got a report from s/v Casablanca that at his position just north of us he was getting wind readings of close to 30 knots. We decided to put a second reef in the main and alter our course for San Juanico - a good windy weather anchorage, but about 30 miles east of our rhumb line to Turtle Bay. Bummer. We had really been hoping to make it much farther on this leg. We were really behind schedule, and I was pretty stressed about it. I knew there wasn't anything that could be done about it, but I was stressed nonetheless. Cruising is much more enjoyable when you aren't on a schedule. And like adding insult to injury, I was missing my dogs terribly, which only served to kick my impatient tendencies into high gear.

From the log, April 16, 2007

After much uncertainty about what the weather was going to do and if the wind was going to lay down, it finally did around 8:15 PM. Just like that. We all decided to beat feet out of San Juanico and see how far we can get by Tuesday night or Wednesday morning. Personally, I'm hoping for Turtle Bay. Then at least we'll feel like we've accomplished something... like we've made it at least half way home.

11:00 PM, Same night... Back on the hook in San Juanico. The conditions were too much.

From the log, April 17, 2007

San Juanico, 166 miles south of Turtle Bay...

That's right. We're stuck here in San Juanico, and from the sounds of the weather reports, it looks like we'll be here until Friday or Saturday. I had hoped and planned to be home by tomorrow, and the reality is we won't be home for at least another 8 or 10 days. We aren't even half way. The wind has consistently been blowing 25-30 knots everyday, right on our nose, causing us to be unable to do in 15 to 20 hours what a car on the highway could do in one hour. This trip is turning out to be one of the most frustrating experiences of my life. I'm home sick, I miss my dogs, and I feel guilty and totally helpless about not meeting my work obligations. I've been crying a lot from the stress of it all. I try not

*to, at least in front of Bryan, because I know he feels bad enough
as it is that he can't make it all better.*

It's pretty ironic, really. In all my years, sailing and being on the ocean
has been my happy place, the place I want to be when the rest of the
world gets me down. At that point in the trip, however, I would have
given almost anything to get off the boat and be back home. I was
really unhappy. I was wishing I could catch a bus from San Juanico
back to California. Unfortunately, that would have left Bryan all
alone out there, and I wouldn't do that to him.

To make matters worse, I had only provisioned for about ten days.
I figured I would get more food in Turtle Bay. We were still doing
okay, but eating a lot less than usual to stretch our supplies. A good
way to drop a few pounds, I guess. Additionally, I didn't bring along
as much cash as I probably should have. We thought we'd only need
to get fuel in Turtle Bay, but as it turned out, we had to get it in Mag
Bay. The trip from Cabo to Mag was so slow and because we were
beating into the current the whole way, we burned a whole tank of
fuel. I was thinking we probably had just enough cash left to fill the
tank in Turtle Bay, but probably not enough for any groceries. As
humbling as it would have been, we were contemplating bumming
a few pesos from Beth and Leonard if we got desperate. Unless, by
some miracle, Turtle Bay had gotten an ATM machine in the previous
18 months, which wasn't the case.

Crazier still is that San Juanico seemed like a pretty cool little
Mexican town. There seemed to be at least a few Americans living
there, drawn by the prospect of good surfing out at the point. There
is a small market and an internet signal that while intermittent, is
still appreciated. Under less stressful conditions I think I could have
been happy spending some time in this pretty Baja cove.

At about noon on Tuesday Paul on s/v Casablanca got anxious and
made a run for it. In his favor was the fact that his boat motors along
at about 7 knots, which is something s/v Godspeed and s/v Salty
Dog couldn't ever hope to accomplish in those conditions. Good for
him, we were thinking. We were really hoping he could make some

progress north. What a trooper he is - as a singlehander, I wouldn't want to be out there if in fact the winds ratcheted up to 30+ knots as forecast. Talk about miserable. Not to mention the threat of breaking something.

During our exile in San Juanico, I kept finding myself wondering how to explain all of the weather drama to our non-sailor friends... After all, it was hard for *me* to come to grips with how trapped we truly were, so I can only imagine what friends at home must have thought. They probably thought that we were sitting in some beautiful anchorage, sipping margaritas, and laughing about how we had them all fooled. Hah. Fat chance. Just for "fun," here's a little list I compiled for them about what life on a sailboat bashing north up the Baja is really like:

1) Bashing up the Baja is... realizing that you won't be able to wash your bed linens until you get to Ensenada, which could be a couple more weeks! Hopefully your boat isn't taking water through the dorade and getting the v berth wet with salt water, since salt water doesn't dry very well. When you're already freezing from your overnight watch, the last thing would want to do is climb into a soggy bunk.

2) Bashing up the Baja is... gaining a new appreciation for modern plumbing. At home, you can shower whenever you want to or need to. This is not always the case on a moving sailboat. Not only could it be hazardous to your health, but you may or may not have hot water, and you know how much fun an ice cold shower is!

3) Bashing up the Baja is... a lesson in conservation. You have to monitor your water consumption every day, especially if you don't have a water maker. But even if you have a water maker, you can't run it all the time or in all conditions, so every drop counts.

4) Bashing up the Baja is... a good way to lose weight. If you run out of food before you get to Turtle Bay, you can't just run to

the store for more! Provisioning well takes on a whole new level of importance, or you may end up like us, eating boxed mashed potatoes and creamed corn more than you ever wanted to.

5) Bashing up the Baja is... Keeping your trash to a minimum, because there may not be anywhere to throw it away for quite awhile. You learn to smash everything down to its smallest size, and stack aluminum cans inside one another like puzzle pieces. And rinse everything before it goes in the trash can, because if it stinks... you have to live with it for awhile!

6) Bashing up the Baja is... Monitoring your fuel consumption carefully, because you won't be able to pull into the service station for more. Out here, you can't just call Vessel Assist if you run out of diesel, so you might as well start sailing for Hawaii, because you won't make it north to Ensenada without a good southerly breeze.

7) Bashing up the Baja is... Being cut off from cell phone service and realizing that you won't die because of it. You'll be lucky if you have signal 25% of the time. You just have to hope your loved ones haven't sent out the Coast Guard since they haven't heard from you in so long.

8) Bashing up the Baja is... a good time to renew your love of reading. At home you have cable TV. On the boat you have movies on the laptop that you watch over and over and over. Either that, or crack the cover on one of those books gathering dust on the shelf.

9) Bashing up the Baja is... cause for dishpan hands. At home you have the luxury of a dishwasher. On the boat, I AM THE DISHWASHER... sometimes three times a day!

10) Bashing up the Baja is... wishing you were more sure-footed. Going to the restroom on a sailboat bashing up the Baja is reminiscent of being in the "Shake Shack" in the carnival scene

in the movie "Grease": The floor is moving up and down, you're trying not to go airborne, and there are lots of interesting things that can happen to you in there. And at home, or even on an airplane, you just flush the toilet after you go, right? On a sailboat bashing up the Baja, flushing the toilet requires serious skills... The ability to stand up and turn around in a small space, brace yourself so you don't go flying, pump the handle with one hand and hold on for dear life with the other.

11) Cooking in those conditions is great fun, as well. Beans are easy - they stick to the pot. Boiling water, on the other hand, is a recipe for disaster. Bashing up the Baja is hoping you won't have reason to put your first aid training to use.

12) Bashing up the Baja is... realizing how much you truly can accomplish on little or no sleep, because you'd probably have better luck sleeping on a roller coaster than on a sailboat doing the Bash in 10 foot swells spaced 8 seconds apart.

13) Bashing up the Baja is... wishing your boat had a pilot house, because it's COLD out there! Prepare to dress like you're vacationing in Alaska. Three layers are not really enough most of the time, especially at night. You certainly don't get to come home from the Bash with a tan. Wind burn maybe, but definitely not a tan.

14) Bashing up the Baja is... a humbling experience. Hopefully you aren't someone who has boasted about never getting seasick. EVERYONE, even the saltiest sailors among us, get a little queasy in the kinds of conditions the Bash can throw at you!

From the log, April 18, 2007, San Juanico

No wind all night. By morning, a slight southerly breeze. By 10 AM, Paul was gone, and by 10:30 AM Salty Dog and Godspeed had also hoisted anchor. What the hell - we won't really know what it's like unless we get out there.

_Not too bad for the first few hours. Pretty choppy from about 1 PM
- 5 PM. Unfortunately, after making grilled cheese sandwiches
for us for dinner, I got a queasy stomach that I couldn't shake
all night long. Bryan pretty much single-handed all the way to
Abreojos. The wind was really shifty, so I did help him with the
tacks, but not much else. Bad first mate._

Around 6 PM that night, we had a brief scare when Paul, s/v
Casablanca, told us he had "bumped" into a shoal. He thought he
was further offshore than he actually was, and got himself into some
pretty shallow waters. It scared the bejesus out of him, but he stayed
extremely calm, and was able to power off the shoal. I'm glad it wasn't
worse, and more importantly, that we were all in the vicinity if he had
needed help.

It got really cold after the sun set, but Captain Bryan was such a
trooper and stayed outside the whole way to Abreojos, letting me
tend to my upset stomach inside the warm boat. I came on deck
about 1:30 AM for the final hour pulling into the dark anchorage.
We got the anchor set, checked in with our buddy boats, and were in
bed by 3 AM.

Abreojos to Turtle Bay

*Y*OU JUST NEVER KNOW WHEN you might need that crazy spare part you're carrying around!

After setting the hook in Abrejos and rolling into our berth around 3 AM, Bryan slept like a log and didn't roll out until 11 AM that morning when there was chatter on the VHF between Paul, Leonard, and Joe. Leonard was antsy to take advantage of the southerly breeze we were getting and make our way to Hipolito, 27 miles north. S/v Salty Dog, s/v Godspeed, and s/v Casablanca weighed anchor at noon. S/v Katy Kat had decided not to leave until after dinner.

> *From the log: 2 PM, same day. First attempt no good. Too rough. Back on the hook by 2 PM. Clocked 29 knots out of the north in the anchorage this afternoon. 11:45 PM Second attempt. Katy Kat went first and said all is well, so the rest of us followed.*
>
> *Underway from Abreojos to Asuncion. Slow going - really strong current. Cold, cold night.*

At 7 AM the next morning I was awakened from a little nap I was taking by Bryan saying rather loudly, "Honey, I need your help! We've got issues!" Uh-oh. In a matter of seconds, I watched from the companionway as he opened the starboard lazaret, took off the radiator cap, and lots of hot, smelly air came rushing out. Bryan said, "I need water, lots of water!" Something was seriously wrong with the radiator. It was bone dry. We kept filling it with 32 ounce bottles of water, but and all the bottles and bottles we would put in it just kept disappearing. The problem was that we couldn't figure out where it was going. We killed the engine and called s/v Godspeed on the VHF. Both boats agreed we would make way to the anchorage at Hipolito.

Now, at this point, you're probably expecting me to say that I started flipping out, having a panic attack or something. But I didn't! For some reason, I was amazingly calm. Maybe because I know by now that the last thing the captain needs in times like these is a first mate/wife who flips her lid during an emergency. The captain of s/v Salty Dog usually problem solves more efficiently when he doesn't have to worry about me, and problem solving was what we needed at that very moment.

Leonard and Bryan both felt the oil needed to be checked to make sure that the water wasn't going into the motor. Bryan can't easily get to the dip stick, buried deep in the port lazaret, and it would be especially difficult underway. So, I crawled in the lazaret myself, wedged myself between the battery boxes and the fuel tank, knees tucked to my chest, and checked the oil. Thankfully, it looked fine. We decided to fire up the engine again and try to make some headway toward Hipolito, all the way filling the radiator reservoir with 32 ounce bottles of water every 8-10 minutes. We did this for about 4 hours, until we finally got to Hipolito.

> About noon... anchor set in Hipolito. With Godspeed and Katy Kat. Nothing here except a few seasonal fishermen's huts. Certainly no boat supplies. But the three local panga fishermen (the ONLY three) did come up to us and ask for an antenna for their VHF. Guess they need parts, too!

Bob Bitchin, the publisher of Latitudes and Attitudes magazine, is well known for saying, "Cruising is just fixing your boat in exotic places." Boy, isn't that the truth!

We got the anchor set, pulled all the stuff out of the lazarets - sail bags, cushions, ditch bag, etc - and began trouble shooting our problem. Again I did boat yoga to get down to the engine where Bryan can't fit, all the while getting greasy and getting my hair stuck on little pieces of fiberglass mesh. Fun. But, it all paid off because we found the problem. A radiator hose had been rubbing against the motor - who knows for how long - and had a puncture in it. Basically, the water we put in the radiator came out that spot as though a faucet

115

was on. After close to an hour of struggling to get the blasted hose off, we finally did, and Bryan took it over to Leonard, who pulled from his endless supply of very necessary boat repair parts exactly what we needed to fix our busted radiator hose.

Now, some people are just naturally gifted when it comes to improvising creative solutions to problems, especially mechanical problems. My husband is gifted like this, but in Leonard he has met his match. In fact, in Leonard he has met his *idol*. Additionally, we all know someone who is a pack rat to the extreme, and we wish we could help those people purge some of the clutter from their lives. As it turns out, our dear friend Leonard is a pack rat, but after the fix he was able to pull off in Hipolito, I will NEVER criticize him for all the stuff he totes around with him in the bowels of his boat.

Bryan and Leonard cut out the bad piece of the hose, and then Leonard cut a piece of bicycle seat post (yes, you read that right!) about 3 inches long with a hacksaw to replace the part they removed. About why he had a bicycle seat post aboard, he said (and I quote), "It had some good steel, and you just never know when it might come in handy." Uh, you mean like today?! Back on s/v Salty Dog, Bryan and I shimmied and wiggled into our various impossible positions to re-fit the hose. After a few adjustments to the length, we got it. We filled up the radiator- again - and fired up the engine. No drips. No disappearing water. Yea!! We really fixed it. Thank you, Leonard, for being a pack rat!

> **TIP: Pack spare parts away in every nook and cranny you can sacrifice. Focus especially on the replacements you know will be hard to find in Mexico. The thing you don't pack will be the one spare part you wish you had!**

We left Hipolito around midnight that same night and arrived in Asuncion the next morning at 6 AM. We set the hook, waited until s/v Godspeed was set, and then went to bed. We lazed around the boat all day, trying to rest and stay warm, and then departed for Turtle Bay at 11 PM.

With much relief and gratitude, we arrived in Turtle Bay around 11 AM. (Did I mention how RELIEVED and GRATEFUL we were?) Within the hour, we had the anchor set and had taken on 54 gallons of diesel from Ruben of "Anabel's Service," who delivers fuel in his panga and pumps it into the tanks of appreciative mariners with a high pressure pump. His ability to do this saves boaters from having to med-tie to the pier in Turtle Bay. If you've seen the pier there, you know that this is no easy undertaking.

S/v Casablanca and s/v Katy Kat were in Turtle Bay, too, so the whole gang went to shore and had lunch and Coronas at Maria's, the little restaurant overlooking the bay (the same place where we had met our friends Rob and Kat 18 months earlier). The food was marginal, but at least we didn't have to cook or clean up! We went to the market in town for provisions, which was as exciting as Christmas. Diet Coke, bread, tortillas, fruit, cereal, chips, and candy. Hooray!! Back on the boat, we talked to our parents on the cell phone (another hooray experience) and napped off and on until 1 AM, when we raised the anchors and headed north.

> *From the log, April 22nd: 6 AM. Back in Turtle Bay. Got outside and after about 2 1/2 hours turned back because of 25 knots on the nose and super large seas. A strong current had us doing only about 2 knots. This sucks.*

Turtle Bay to Ensenada
Almost home...

WE ENDED UP SPENDING ANOTHER three days in Turtle Bay, trying to keep a positive attitude and trying to keep ourselves entertained. We finally departed on April 25th at 8 PM. It was a terrible night, possibly the worst of the trip. We had worried it might be like this, but it seemed to be the only marginally safe weather window we were going to have for another ten days or so. We suffered through 20 knots on the nose, big, lumpy seas, and freezing cold temperatures. Neither of us was able to sleep for the first 24 hours - a first for us. We would have liked to, but the conditions made it impossible. We spent the daylight hours avoiding kelp to the best of our ability and trying to maneuver through the swells in such a way as to keep from breaking something. We were exhausted, soaked to the bone, and a little scared.

By the middle of the afternoon on the second day, we were on the outside of Cedros Island and conditions finally improved enough for Bryan to get about 3 1/2 hours of rest. I woke him around 8 PM for some dinner, and then he went on watch so I could sleep. For the next 18 hours, we were able to keep a regular watch schedule. The swells were at least 14', but far enough apart to be manageable and comfortable. There was no sun, though; cloudy skies kept the temperatures cold, and we remained bundled up in multiple layers of clothing and foul weather gear.

> From the log, April 28th: It's been about 36 hours since my last log entry, and amazingly, we are now within 3 hours of Ensenada. Thank the Lord! The last 36 hours have been pretty fair, other than the June gloom that has kept the sun away and kept the temps really cold. STILL in foulies. Can't wait to burn them.

Last night we had a scary episode. I napped from 10 PM - 2 AM, and when I awoke and removed my ear plug from my right ear, I felt an excruciating pain inside my ear. When I tried to move to the companionway to get Bryan's attention, I began to feel like I was going to faint. I had just enough time to tell him what I was feeling before I blacked out and went limp. He says he sat me down on the bench and as soon as I started to come to, I fainted again. When I came to the second time, I had the cold sweats. He got me outside for some fresh air, which helped, but of course then I was freezing and started shivering like crazy. Long story short, Bryan thinks my equilibrium was all screwed up from being underway for the last 3 1/2 days, wearing my two seasick bands, and only one ear plug while sleeping. (Doing so helps convince me that I'll be able to hear Bryan if he's hollering for me). He let me go back to sleep since I was feeling pretty rotten, and when I got up around 5:30 AM I was much better. Glad that's all it was. Pretty scary, though.

Today we napped off and on, talked to Ma and Pa Godspeed on the radio, and I finished another book, my fifth of the trip. This afternoon we were visited by a cute little yellow bird who decided to take up temporary residence on the leg of Bryan's yellow foulies, which he was wearing at the time. Eventually the bird left, but he must have gone and told all his friends about us because soon we had 5 or 6 yellow birds hitching a ride on Salty Dog. We thought we had shooed them all away, only to discover one asleep on the spigot of the galley sink, and another asleep on top of the medicine cabinet in the head, having apparently flown in through the open porthole. Cute for awhile - of course, we took some pictures - but a pain to get rid of! Stubborn little brats had us trying to coax them out of every possible hatch and porthole for about an hour.

Just south of Ensenada, it seemed appropriate to summarize what we thought of the trip north. Well, I can honestly say that renaming the Baja Bash the "Baja Bliss" didn't work out as we all had hoped. It ended up taking us 21 days to do what we hoped to accomplish in 10-14, and we were only able to make it to Ensenada in that amount of time. Bryan still had to bring the boat the rest of the way to Long Beach, which would end up taking another two weeks due to the weather.

Yes, the weather was consistently bad. Every passage was miserably cold. I was queasy a lot of the trip - which doesn't usually happen to me. There isn't much good I can say about the experience - I certainly wouldn't choose to do it again. However, we have been told since our return home that possibly we just timed our trip poorly, which is possible. If you don't mind the fog of the early spring, May or June may potentially be a better time of year to bash.

The only thing that helped make the trip bearable was being with Beth and Leonard, and the new friends we made along the way- Joe and Kathy, and Paul. Without friends to commiserate and socialize with, we probably would have lost our minds! But hey, to us, the best part about cruising has always been the people you meet along the way.

And as miserable as the trip was, now we can say with pride that... WE SURVIVED THE BAJA BASH!!

here comes
colder winds and the changing tides
we better drop them sails and come inside
when will the weather ever let us go
i guess we'll have to wait until the trade winds blow
and we'll be

free

Lyrics from "Free" by Donovan Frankenreiter

Chapter 9

Final Thoughts

NOW THAT WE HAVE BEEN home for awhile, we find it interesting that people are still asking us about our trip. So many people, boaters and non-boaters alike, want to hear about our Mexico sailing adventure. They want to hear us tell of the good times and the not-so-good times. And inevitably, they always ask us if we would do it again.

Without hesitation, we both say that we would make the trip again, and that there have been many, many days since our return to California when we in fact have found ourselves yearning for the simplicity of our cruising days. If you have read this story in its entirety, you know that many days were difficult, especially the trip back up the Baja. We acknowledge those difficulties for what they were, yet still feel that the cruising lifestyle offers something to adventure-seekers and those who desire to be truly self-reliant that most other lifestyles cannot.

Despite the difficulties, we are extremely proud of the fact that we took a leap of faith and decided to fulfill our dream. It didn't seem right, however, to finish out the story of our Mexico cruising adventure with our story of the Bash. We thought we should end on something a little more, well... positive. The Bash was tough, but there is so much about our cruising adventure that was wonderful, and we want to recap those things here. In closing, we felt it fitting to highlight some of the rewards and lessons we picked up from various latitudes along the way.

1) Lesson: Appreciate the freedom and independence as long as it lasts. No alarm clock (except the watch alarm!), no schedule except the one you set for yourselves, and the chance to go where you want, when you want.

2) Lesson: Always carry spare parts! If you have the spare, the part won't break. *If you don't have the spare, well... we'll keep our fingers crossed for you!*

3) Lesson: It is best to over provision on food and drinks, and carry more cash than you think you will need. You just can't

predict what may happen and where you may be marooned...
Los Frailes, Mag Bay, Turtle Bay. You get the idea.

4) Lesson: Unless you have a money tree onboard, stay out of marinas as much as possible. They'll make you poor!

5) Lesson: Remember KISS- Keep It Simple, Stupid! The simpler the system, the easier it will be to fix when it breaks.

6) Lesson: Have a good sense of humor. It will come in handy when something *does* break, or when the weather is bad, or when something unforeseen messes up your plans (which will happen at least a few times!)

7) Lesson: Enjoy yourself, but don't become a "drunken sailor." Unfortunately, this happens to a lot of cruisers, and it is really sad to see.

8) Reward: Savor the remote, beautiful anchorages and the tranquility they offer. Commit them to memory. When you're back home and back at work, memories of the time you spent in these places can help get you through the toughest of days.

9) Reward: Appreciate the characters you meet and the wonderful friends you make... You will soon find yourself reflecting on all the great times you had with these people, the lessons you learned from them, and how blessed you feel to have connected with them during such a pivotal time in your life.

10) Reward: The sense of pride you will feel for having the courage to do it... the courage to cut the docklines and live out your dream.

Appendix A

S/V Salty Dog's

Favorite Cruising Recipes

First and foremost...
COCKTAILS!

Buffalo Milk

Fill blender 3/4 ¾ full with ice. Pour equal parts vodka, Crème de Banana, Dark Crème de Cocoa (+/- 3 ounces each). Add milk to top of ice and blend. Pour into glasses, top off with whipped cream and a drizzle of Kahlua. Sprinkle with nutmeg.

Landfall Daiquiri

1 banana

7 ounces canned peaches and/or pineapple

6 to 8 ounces rum

2 tablespoons sugar

Juice of ½ lime or lemon

½ 1 / 2 teaspoon of vanilla extract

Nutmeg or fresh mint (if available!) for garnish

Place ingredients in blender, mix until thick, add ice, blend again until even thicker. Garnish and celebrate!

(recipe courtesy of Cruising World, August 2003)

BUSHWHACKER

(Carrie's personal BVI favorite!)
Rum, Vodka, Bailey's, Kahlua, Amaretto, Frangelico, crème de cocoa,
and milk. Blend until smooth.

RUM PUNCH

A healthy mix of rum, and any combination of the following juices:
orange, pineapple, mango, lime. Add a splash of grenadine if you
have it.

BAJA MARGARITA

Mix 2 parts premium gold tequila, 2 parts some other tequila, 1 part
Controy in a glass with ice. Fill to the top with fresh squeezed lime
juice. Stir in I tablespoon sugar.

Additionally, any well stocked cruising vessel will have available the following for their guests:

Red wine

White wine

Vodka

Rum

Whiskey

Tequila

Tonic

Coke/Diet Coke

Sprite/ 7-Up

Cranberry Juice

Orange Juice

Note: Some of these items may also come in handy for trading with the locals!

And to go with your cocktails....

SNACKS!!

GUACAMOLE

2-3 ripe avocados

1 ripe tomato (optional)

1 / 4 onion, chopped

2 limes or lemons

Mash together

Add cumin, chili powder, garlic salt to taste

OR

Hot sauce to taste

SALSA

3-4 large tomatoes

Chop together 1 bunch cilantro and 1 medium brown onion

1-2 yellow chilies

1 green jalapeno

1-2 serrano chilies

tomatillos (optional)

½ 1 /2 cup beer

Oregano, salt, garlic salt to taste

Squeeze lime or lemon juice over all ingredients. Let sit for at least
one half hour so flavors can blend.

Mango Salsa

1 ripe mango, diced
Red bell pepper
Jalapeno
Red onion
Lime juice
Basil
Salt & Pepper
(Great over blackened fish!)

Ceviche

Approx. 1 pound white fish, uncooked and chunked
Juice of 6-8 limes
2-3 ripe tomatoes (or less if you prefer)
3 jalapeno or Serrano chilies, deseeded & sliced
1 /2 teaspoon dried oregano
1 / 3 cup extra virgin olive oil
1 small white onion, finely chopped
salt and pepper

Marinate fish in lime juice. Chill for at least 5 hours. Mix occasionally. (Fish must turn opaque). About 1 hour before serving, mix fish with remainder of ingredients. About 15 minutes before serving, remove from fridge. Serve with saltines or tortilla chips.

Tips:

Because it's hard to come by in some places of the world, like Mexico, sour cream-based dips always seem to be a crowd pleaser. Serve with crackers and/or veggies. Stock your galley with dip mixes, onion soup mix, etc. www.tastefullysimple.com is a great source for these items.

Additionally, melted Velveeta can be mixed with a variety of ingredients (sausage, jalapenos, diced tomatoes, etc) and served with tortilla chips.

And now, for the

MAIN COURSE

Pressure Cooker Lobster

Open a can of beer and let it go flat. Once accomplished, pour the beer into the bottom of your pressure cooker. Insert the basket or rack. Place cleaned lobsters on the rack. Lock the lid and bring to pressure, then cook for 6 more minutes. Remove from stove and submerse the bottom half of the pressure cooker in cold water in the sink. Serve steamed lobster with lemon wedges, and if desired, melted butter.

Lobster Tails on the Grill

1. Clean lobster and pat dry with paper towels. Butterfly tails by using kitchen shears or a sharp knife to cut lengthwise through the centers of hard top shells and meat, cutting to, but not through, bottoms of shells. Press shell halves apart with your fingers.

2. Lightly grease the rack of a gas grill. Preheat, then reduce heat to medium. Brush lobster meat with melted butter. Place lobster, meat side down, on the grill directly over heat. Cover and grill 6 minutes, or until meat is opaque. Turn lobster, brush with more melted butter. Squeeze fresh lemon juice over them if you wish. Cook 6 more minutes.

(DO NOT OVERCOOK or your
lobster will be tough and chewy. What a shame!)

CITRUS CHICKEN

Any combination of chicken pieces (we prefer boneless, skinless breasts)
Oranges, Lemons, Limes, and/or orange juice
Salt and Pepper

Reserve 1-2 whole lemons. Marinate the chicken in the juices of the citrus fruits for a minimum of 2 hours, or preferably, overnight.

Grill chicken, lightly sprinkling with salt and pepper. Throughout grilling time, squeeze the juice of the remaining 1-2 lemons over chickens.

Note: If you don't have time to marinate, baste with a mixture of orange juice, and the juice of fresh lemons and limes while bbq-ing.

CHILI-RUBBED PORK CHOPS (OR PORK KEBABS)

Boneless pork loin chops
(Whole or cut into 1-inch cube pieces for kebabs)
3 Tablespoons Chili Powder
1 Teaspoon Kosher Salt
1 - 2 Tablespoons Olive Oil
1 /4 Teaspoon Freshly Ground Black Pepper

Combine chili powder and salt in a large bowl. Add the pork and the oil and toss to coat. Grill, turning regularly, until cooked through.

(Recipe courtesy of Real Simple magazine)

OPTIONAL PINEAPPLE SALSA
FOR CHILI-RUBBED PORK

1 pineapple, peeled and cut crosswise into 1 / 2 –inch-thick slices

1 jalapeno, seeded and finely chopped

1 cup roughly chopped fresh cilantro

1 Tablespoon fresh lime juice

1 Tablespoon Olive Oil

3/ 4 teaspoon salt

Pepper

Grill the pineapple for approximately 2 minutes per side on a preheated medium-high grill. Cut into small, diced pieces, discarding the core. In a bowl, combine the pineapple, jalapeno, cilantro, lime juice, oil, salt, and black pepper. Serve over pork or any blackened fish.

ONE POT PASTA

1 12-oz. package spiral pasta

2 16-oz. cans stewed tomatoes

1 10-oz can chicken broth

Olive oil

Italian seasoning

Bring all ingredients except pasta to a boil. Add pasta. Cover and simmer 16-18 minutes. Stir twice.

Tuna Noodle Casserole

6 oz. cooked noodles

1 can tuna, drained (2 cans if you prefer more tuna flavor)

1 can cream of celery or cream of mushroom soup

1 / 2 cup milk

1 cup grated cheddar cheese

1 / 2 cup mayo

1 / 2 cup diced celery

1 / 3 cup chopped onion

1 / 4 cup chopped, canned pimiento

1 / 2 teaspoon salt

Mix soup and 1 / 2 cup milk in a large skillet, heat through. Add 1 cup grated cheddar; heat and stir until cheese melts. In a casserole dish, mix cooked noodles, tuna, mayo, celery, onion, pimientos, and salt. Add cheese mixture to noodle mixture. Stir well. Bake uncovered at 425 degrees for 20 minutes.

Spaghetti with Clam Sauce

2 / 3 + lbs spaghetti

2 6.5-oz. cans chopped (or diced) clams

2-3 cloves diced garlic

1 ½ 1 / 2 Tablespoons Flour

Margarine

Parsley (if you've got it aboard!)

Thyme

Salt & Pepper

Melt 3 1/ 2 Tablespoons margarine in a skillet. Add garlic and flour. Stir. Add clams and their juice. Stir until somewhat thickened. Add

2 Tablespoons parsley, a little thyme, salt and pepper. Serve over cooked and buttered spaghetti.

CHICKEN TORTILLA CASSEROLE

3 small cans salsa verde

5 cups shredded cooked chicken, skinned

1 cup sour cream

1 / 2 cup whipping cream (can substitute whole milk)

12 corn tortillas, cut into 1 / 4 inch wide strips

3 1 / 2 cups firmly packed shredded cheddar

1 / 3 cup grated parmesan (if you've got it)

1 large avocado, thinly sliced (for garnish)

Place half the chicken in a 9x13 baking dish. Spread with half the salsa. Mix sour cream and whipping cream and spread half the mixture over salsa. Top with half the tortilla strips and half the cheddar cheese. Repeat layers, using remaining ingredients. Cover and bake at 350 degrees for 40 minutes. Uncover, and continue baking 5 more minutes. Remove from oven. Let stand for 10 minutes. Arrange avocado slices on top of casserole. Makes 7-8 servings.

Tip: There are plenty of roadside stands in Mexico that cook rotisserie chicken all day long. This type of chicken works great in this recipe.

ONE PAN TACO DINNER

1 lb. ground beef

Taco seasoning (or whip up your own spice combo)

2 cups Minute white rice, uncooked

1 cup shredded cheddar cheese

2 cups shredded lettuce (optional)

1 large tomato, diced

Brown meat in a large skillet; drain. Add 2 cups water and seasonings; stir. Bring to a boil. Stir in rice. Sprinkle with cheese; cover. Cook on low heat 5 minutes. Top with lettuce and tomato just before serving.

Great served with tortilla chips instead of forks!

Chicken Enchiladas with Green Sauce

Enchilada Sauce

4 cups shredded chicken (canned works well if fresh isn't available)

3 cups shredded jack cheese

1 large can diced green chilies

2 teaspoons dried oregano

Salt

Vegetable oil

Corn tortillas

Sour cream

Fresh chopped cilantro (optional)

1. In a large bowl, mix chicken, 2 cups cheese, chilies, and oregano. Season to taste with salt. 2. Pour oil into frying pan. Fry each tortilla just until limp (about 10 seconds each side). Drain on paper towels. 3. While tortillas are warm, spoon 1 / 2 cup of the chicken mixture in each. Roll and place seam-side down in baking dish.

4. Cover with foil and bake at 350 degrees until hot in center (about 20 minutes). Uncover and top with remaining cheese. Continue baking uncovered until cheese is melted.

CHICKEN PARMESAN

4 skinned, boneless chicken breast halves

1 egg, lightly beaten

1 / 3 cup Italian-seasoned breadcrumbs

2 Tablespoons butter or margarine

1 3 / 4 cups spaghetti sauce

1 / 2 cup shredded mozzarella

1 Tablespoon grated Parmesan cheese

1. Place chicken between 2 sheets plastic wrap; flatten to 1 / 4 inch thickness using a meat mallet or rolling pin. 2. Dip chicken in egg; dredge in crumbs. 3. Melt butter in a skillet over medium-high heat; add chicken and cook 2 minutes on each side or until browned. 4. Pour spaghetti sauce over chicken. Cover, reduce heat, and simmer 10 minutes. Sprinkle with cheeses. Cover and simmer 5 more minutes or until cheese melts.

(from Cooking Light magazine)

Side Dishes

Mom's Corn Casserole

1 17-oz. can cream-style corn

1 4-oz. can diced green chiles

1 4-oz. jar diced pimientos, drained

1 / 2 cup butter

2 eggs, beaten

1 / 2 cup cornmeal

1 / 2 teaspoon salt

1 cup sour cream

2 cups shredded jack cheese

Place all ingredients in a large bowl and mix with a spoon. Turn into greased 1 1 / 2 quart baking dish (preferably shallow). Bake uncovered at 375 degrees for 40 minutes or until set. Makes 4 – 6 servings.

Parmesan Zucchini

2 large zucchini, thinly sliced

2 teaspoons olive oil

2 cloves garlic, minced

parmesan cheese

margarine

Heat the oil in a skillet over medium heat. Cook zucchini and garlic in oil until zucchini softens to the texture you prefer. Melt small spoonfuls of margarine over the veggies. Sprinkle with parmesan cheese and toss well to coat. Cook until cheese becomes slightly browned.

CREAMY MUSHROOM RICE

Prepare 2 cups instant white rice following directions on box, but substitute 1 can cream of mushroom soup and 1 1 / 2 cups water for the 2 cups of water in the regular directions. Stir in 1 small jar or can of drained sliced mushrooms. Add lots of pepper and as much salt as you prefer.

TUNA ELBOW SALAD

Half of a 1 lb package of elbow macaroni

1 / 2 cup mayo

3 tablespoons milk

2 tablespoons vinegar

1 / 2 teaspoon sugar

generous additions of salt and pepper

3 hard boiled eggs, chopped

1 / 2 cup chopped celery

1 / 3 cup finely chopped onion

1 can tuna, drained

Cook macaroni and drain well. In a large bowl, stir together mayo, milk, vinegar, sugar, salt and pepper. Add remaining ingredients; mix well. Cover, chill thoroughly.

Tip: This is a great dish to take to a cruiser's potluck. However, it sometimes turns out a little too bland. This can be solved by making sure you've added enough vinegar, sugar, salt and pepper.

Tip: This is also a great make-ahead salad for a long passage that can be easily served if conditions are too rough for preparing sandwiches, etc.

Breads and Desserts

Easy Beer Bread

(Recipe courtesy of Leonard Wahlquist, "Pa Godspeed")

3 cups self-rising flour

3 tbsp sugar

1 12oz. can beer

Mix all ingredients in a large mixing bowl; dough will be lumpy. Pour into a greased loaf pan and bake at 375 degrees for 40-45 minutes. As soon as it comes out of the oven, brush the top with melted butter.

Tip: You can vary this recipe by adding dried rosemary, parmesan cheese, or shredded cheddar cheese to the dry mixture.

Italian Bread (Sponge recipe)

While this recipe may seem complicated, it really isn't, although it does take a good part of the day to make the bread. Be sure you have a big surface on which to roll out the dough... we used our dinette table.

We acquired this recipe from our friend Kelly aboard s/v S/v Moorea when we spent time together in La Paz. She had experimented with many, many bread recipes to ensure she had a good one for their month –long crossing from Mexico to the South Pacific. She was right, this is a good one, and will make your whole boat smell delicious!

Part 1:

1 cup lukewarm water

1 1/ 2 cups all-purpose flour

1 1 / 2 teaspoons active dry yeast

Combine flour and yeast in a mixing bowl. Stir in the water. Mixture will be very thick. Cover with plastic wrap or a dish towel. Let sit at room temperature 4 – 12 hours (12 hours max!)

Part 2:

3 tablespoons lukewarm water

1 1 / 2 teaspoons salt

1 3 / 4 cups all-purpose flour

Add water and salt to sponge. Stir in the flour, adding an extra tablespoon or two of flour if dough seems sticky. With floured hands, knead until smooth, approx 8 minutes. Place in a greased bowl and cover with plastic wrap. Let rise until doubled in size, approx. 1 1 / 2 hours.

Part 3:

Punch the dough down and divide in half. Shape into 2 rectangles. Roll one rectangle from the long side and pinch the seam together. Repeat with the other rectangle. Leave on work surface and cover with plastic wrap (or towels) for 30 minutes.

Part 4:

Preheat oven to 425 degrees. Grease a baking sheet with shortening. Stretch each loaf gently as you place on baking sheet. Sprinkle lightly with flour. Cover and let sit 20 minutes. Cut 3 or 4 slashes across each loaf. Bake approx. 20 minutes. Cool 15 minutes before slicing.

Mama Trilli's Pizza Dough
(courtesy of Gail Anderson, s/v Simplicity)

1 cup warm water

1 packet yeast

3 cups flour

1 / 4 teaspoon salt

1 / 4 cup olive oil

1 tablespoon honey

Mix water, yeast, and 1 cup flour in a bowl. Mix lightly. Let rest for 10 minutes. Add oil and remaining flour. Sprinkle salt on top. Mix. Knead until smooth (approximately 8 minutes). Let rise approximately 1 1 / 2 hour. Punch down. Shape, making sure the crust isn't too thick or it won't cook all the way through without burning on the bottom. (A 9x13 pan can be used in place of a pizza pan). Rest 5 – 10 minutes. Brush edges with olive oil. Add toppings of your choosing. Bake 10 minutes at 425 degrees.

Zucchini Bread

3 eggs

1 cup vegetable oil

2 cups white sugar

2 cups grated zucchini

2 teaspoons vanilla extract

1 / 2 cup chopped walnuts (optional)

1 teaspoon salt

1 / 4 teaspoon baking powder

3 cups all-purpose flour

4 teaspoons ground cinnamon

1 teaspoon baking soda

1 / 2 teaspoon nutmeg

Preheat oven to 325 degrees. Grease and flour 2 loaf pans. In a large bowl, beat eggs until light and frothy. Mix in oil and sugar. Stir in zucchini and vanilla. Combine flour, cinnamon, soda, baking powder, salt, nutmeg, and nuts. Stir into the egg mixture. Divide batter into pans. Bake for 60 – 70 minutes. Makes 2 loaves!

CINNAMON SWIRL BREAD

1 / 3 cup sugar

2 teaspoons ground cinnamon

2 cups all-purpose flour

1 tablespoon baking powder

1 / 2 teaspoon salt

1 cup sugar

1 egg, beaten

1 cup milk

1 / 3 cup vegetable oil

Preheat oven to 350 degrees. Lightly grease a 9x5 loaf pan. In a small bowl, mix together 1 / 3 cup sugar and 2 teaspoons cinnamon; set aside. In a large bowl, combine flour, baking powder, salt and remaining 1 cup sugar. Combine egg, milk, and oil; add to flour mixture. Stir until moistened. Pour half of the batter into pan. Sprinkle with half the reserved cinnamon/sugar mixture. Repeat with remaining batter and cinnamon/sugar mixture. Draw a knife through the batter to marble. Bake in a preheated oven for 45 minutes, or until knife inserted near the center comes out clean. Let cool in pan for 10 minutes, remove to rack and let cool completely.

Tip: A streusel cinnamon nut topping would be good added to this bread.

☙

PUMPKIN PIE

2 cups canned pumpkin

1 15-oz. can sweetened condensed milk

1 egg, beaten

1 / 2 teaspoon salt

1 / 2 teaspoon nutmeg

1 / 2 teaspoon ginger

1 tablespoon cinnamon

Blend together all ingredients in a bowl. Turn mixture into an unbaked pie crust. Bake at 375 degrees approx. 50 minutes, or until sharp knife inserted near the center comes our clean. Refrigerate at least 1 hour.

BANANA BREAD

1 3 / 4 cups all-purpose flour

2 teaspoons baking powder

1 / 4 teaspoon baking soda

1 / 2 teaspoon salt

2 / 3 cup sugar

1 / 3 cup butter, softened

2 eggs

1 cup mashed banana

1 / 2 cup chopped walnuts

2 teaspoons cinnamon

1 / 2 teaspoon nutmeg

Grease a 8x4 loaf pan. Preheat oven to 350 degrees. In a large mixing bowl, sift together flour, baking powder, baking soda, salt, sugar, cinnamon, and nutmeg. Add butter, eggs, nuts, and mashed banana. Beat until well blended. Pour batter into prepared pan and bake about 1 hour.

Hint: While this recipe calls for a mixer and a sifter, I didn't have either aboard and the bread turned out just fine!

Pumpkin Bread

1 cup canned pumpkin

1 / 2 cup vegetable oil

1 1 / 3 cups sugar

2 eggs

1 1 / 2 cups all-purpose flour

1 / 2 teaspoon baking powder

1 / 2 teaspoon baking soda

1/ 2 teaspoon salt

1 / 2 teaspoon cinnamon

1 / 2 teaspoon nutmeg

1 / 2 teaspoon ground cloves

In a large bowl, mix together the pumpkin, oil, sugar and eggs. Combine the flour, baking powder, soda, salt and spices; stir into pumpkin mixture until well blended. Pour into greased 9x5 loaf pan. Bake at 350 degrees for 45-60 minutes, or until top of loaf springs back when lightly pressed.

Appendix B

Provisioning Tips

W HAT FOLLOWS IS A LIST of basic items you will want to stock your vessel with for your cruising adventure. Items in **bold** print are things we used a lot of, and items with an asterisk (*) are hard-to-find outside of the U.S.

(Thanks to Jody of Latitudes & Attitudes magazine for the original version of this list.)

BAKING & MISC

Baking Powder
Baking Soda
All-purpose flour
Self-rising flour
White sugar
Brown sugar
Yeast (self-rising)
Brownie and cake mixes
Frosting
Raisins
Nuts
Sweetened condensed milk
Canned pumpkin
*Bread crumbs
*Corn meal
Cooking spray
Vegetable oil
Olive oil
Honey

HERBS & SPICES

Black pepper
Chili powder
Cumin
Bay leaves
Lemon pepper
Italian seasoning

Garlic salt
Garlic powder
Mexican/taco seasoning
Basil
Oregano
Thyme
Rosemary
*Sage
*Dried parsley
Cinnamon
Nutmeg
*Ginger
*Cloves

SAUCES & CONDIMENTS

*Salad dressings (other than Ranch or Italian, your other favorites will be hard to come by!)

BBQ Sauce
Cheese Wiz
Hot sauce
Tabasco
*Horseradish
Ketchup
Mayo
*Relish
Mustards (regular, Dijon, etc)
Soy Sauce
Worcester
Vinegars (balsamic, white, cider, red wine)

CANNED GOODS

Baked beans
Refried beans
*Chili beans
*Kidney beans

*White beans
Canned fruit
*Canned chicken
Tuna
*Canned clams
Olives
Corn
Green beans
*Stewed tomatoes
Diced tomatoes
Tomato sauce
Salsa verde
Ortega chilies
Enchilada sauce
Spaghetti sauce
Chicken broth
Chicken noodle soup
Tomato soup
Cream of mushroom soup

DRY GOODS

Coffee filters
Birthday candles
Cupcake papers
Crackers
Cookies
Cereal
Jelly
Peanut butter
Popcorn
Pasta
Rice (brown, white)
*Tea (reg, decaf, lemon, Good Earth spice tea)
Coffee
Hot chocolate
Crystal light

LAUNDRY & CLEANING SUPPLIES

*Woolite
Bleach
*Wrinkle spray
*Febreeze
*Lint roller and refills
Simple Green
Toilet bowl cleaner
*Swifter and Swifter refills (wet and dry)
Windex
Air freshener (spray, Plug-ins, candles, etc)

PERSONAL ITEMS

Sunscreen (take your favorites... you won't find them once you get there!)
Chapstick w/ SPF
*Skin So Soft
*Shampoo & Conditioner (take your favorites)
*Detangler/Leave-in conditioner
Deodorant
*Face wash
*Face lotion
*Eye makeup remover
Shaving cream
Razors
Nail polish remover
Nail file/clippers
*Pumice stone
*Hair cutting scissors
Tweezers
Cotton balls
Q-tips
*Ear Plugs

FIRST AID, VITAMINS & MEDICINES

BandAids
Neosporene
Beesting kit (if necessary)
Magnifying glass
Eye drops
Lysine
Multivitamin
Allergy medicine/Benadryl
Dayquil
Nyquil
Motrin
Gaviscon
Simply Sleep

FROM YOUR PHYSICIAN:

Compozine (for severe sea sickness)
Antibiotics
All of your prescriptions
Copies of all prescriptions with physician's contact information

PET SUPPLIES

*Cat food
*Cat litter
Dog treats
Dog food
Refill bags for "Bags on Board" dispenser
Pet First Aid book

Glossary

Arrachera:	Marinated, grilled flank steak
Azul:	Blue
Bonita:	A fish commonly caught off of Baja, California
Booby:	Small marine bird that breeds along rocky coasts and cliffs. Body is generally dark brown on top with white underparts, distinctively colored feet, and pale iris blue eyes.
Carne Asada:	A type of flat meat (beef), usually grilled
Cerveza:	Beer
Ceviche:	Raw white fish marinated in citrus juice (usually lime juice), served with chips or crackers
Chart Plotter:	An electronic instrument that displays charts and positions of various locations, anchorages, coves, marinas and hazards
Cockpit:	An open well aft in a small sailboat at which the helmsman sits to steer, and which offers some protection and safety for the crew
Dinghy:	A small boat carried on a larger vessel as a launch or lifeboat, usually powered by oars, sail, or small outboard motor
Docklines:	Ropes specifically made up for use when securing the vessel to the dock or slip
Dorade:	An air intake on deck, often horn shaped, which brings fresh air below for ventilation to quarters or engine areas

"Foulies":	Rain slicker, waterproof hat and boots and any other such personal clothing that protects a seaman from the cold and wet
Grib Files:	GRIB (GRIdded Binary) is a mathematically concise data format commonly used in meteorology to store historical and forecasted weather data; available to boaters with necessary computer software as a route planning tool
Gringo:	A Westerner, a Yankee
Knot Meter:	An electronic instrument which measures the vessel's speed through the water
Lazaret:	A storage locker (On Salty Dog, located in the cockpit)
Malecon:	Jetty or breakwater, often a popular public area
Manana:	Tomorrow
Marineros:	Mariners, boaters
Muertos:	The dead, the deceased
Palapa:	A shaded patio or shaded sitting area: An open-sided dwelling with a thatched roof made of dried palm leaves
Panaderia:	Bakery, bread shop
Panga:	A skiff or tender; often used in Latin America as a fishing vessel
Porthole:	An opening in the topsides or deck structures that allow light in, and which may be opened for fresh air. Portholes are usually small, with a sturdy hinged

glass cover called a portlight, that can be dogged shut against a watertight gasket

Provisioning: Stocking a vessel with necessary food, drink, and personal items

Pumpouts: Suction device designed to allow contents of holding tank to be removed at the dock and sent to a treatment plant

Rhumb Line: A course line that follows a single heading

Tortillaria: Tortilla shop

Ventana: Window

Verde: Green

Weather Fax: An electronic download of weather data available to boaters using a combination of HAM radio and laptop computer

About the Authors

BRYAN AND CARRIE BERSHEE HAVE spent most of their lives sailing the waters of Southern California with their families. When they met in 1998, they had a mutual dream of owning their own sailboat. Soon after they married in 2000, they purchased their first boat, a 27' Ericson. After a year of trying to accommodate two adults and two dogs on a small sloop, they upgraded to a 1979 Pearson 365 ketch, the same boat they cruised to Mexico.

After a year of living aboard, cruising Baja, and writing their story, Bryan and Carrie have returned to California and are back working in the public school system – Bryan teaching PE and Outdoor Education, and Carrie as a school counselor working with junior high and high school students. They enjoy sailing Salty Dog in her home waters, camping, skiing, and spending time with their two dogs, Fletcher and Sadie. They love the cruising lifestyle and hope to set sail again someday... the destination is yet to be determined. Stay tuned for updates at: www.saltydogadventures.com.

Printed in the United States
118222LV00004B/124-132/P